INTRODUCTION

(OR, "DO NOT SKIP THIS!")

First of all, thanks for buying my book. I know you have a lot of different places you can be spending money, and I'm grateful you thought my book was worth a few of your hard-earned bucks. I've done my best to pack this thing with an embarrassingly rich amount of good information that'll help you get the job you want.

But to do that, I have to be direct and cut through a lot of old, bad information. Some of the advice in this book will be very surprising to you. Like, for instance, the part where I tell you to delete the entire "Objective" portion of your resume, and the part where I rant about people who make the giant "References Available Upon Request" mistake. There's more. It's all in here.

I'm not a sugar coater when it comes to things that can make or break your search for gainful employment. I know how hard it is to get a job, let alone one that pays great money and makes you excited to go to work every morning. Because of this, I'm passionate and direct, and I'll always tell you exactly what I think.

It pisses me off when I see young people coming out of school — where they very likely incurred a lifetime of debts exceeding $100,000 to get what was supposed to be a decent education — and sending out resumes rife with mistakes, lacking critical information and full of other information that no one cares about. It doesn't make me mad at the students; it makes me mad at the schools.

The amount of money students pay to attend college is staggering. Millions of students sign their lives away to crushing debt to get a decent job — at the time of this writing, there is over $1 trillion in outstanding student-loan debt in the US — and most colleges can't be bothered to teach them ANYTHING about the process of getting a job. Just think about that for a second. You are now reading a $5 book in a day or two that will teach you more about how to get a job than most colleges will teach you in four years and $100,000. Or $250,000. Or God-knows-what you paid for that degree you're getting.

That is seriously fucked up. It's a fatally broken piece of the system that no one seems to be paying much attention to, so I decided to fix it myself by writing this book. Of course, I'm just one writer and I can't fix it for everyone, but if you're reading this sentence, I can fix it for you.

You may have already noticed that I swear a lot. I use a lot of crude language. If such language offends you, you should go back to Amazon. com right now and request a refund. They'll give it to you, no questions asked. But this is how I (and, you'll find, a great many others, even in the most highfalutin' professional fields) actually talk in real life. I see no value whatsoever in softening my words and pretending to be something I'm not in order to appease librarians and grandmas. After all, librarians already have jobs so they don't need this book, and your grandma is probably retired. Or, in this economy, already working a couple of side jobs to supplement her Social Security.

Anyhow, because of this, some of my critics have called me rude, insensitive, arrogant, vulgar and other nastier terms. That's OK. I'm occasionally guilty of all those things. Usually the people who knock me are students who have never had a full-time job or teachers and parents who have never been in charge of hiring anyone for anything. I respect everyone's right to their opinion — I'm just pretty well convinced that my opinion is usually right. Hey, that's what makes it *my opinion*, right?

Here's a little about me and why you should listen to me:

I started teaching online resume writing when I was a grad student at the University of Missouri School of Journalism. Those were the days of, by today's standards, painfully tacky HTML resumes that used all kinds of unfortunate colors and lines and gray backgrounds and things that blinked and things that flashed. After I graduated, I was in charge of hiring employees or interns at every job I had. Then I started an advertising agency in 2001 and grew it into a successful company that I still run today.

So I've been on the hiring side of this process plenty of times — more than enough to dish out the advice that fills this book. But I can also clearly remember being on the other side of this process, when I was applying for internships and jobs.

And I empathize with you for all the advice and guidance you're not getting from those around you. If you're lucky, your high school or college may have devoted a whopping one or two class periods to showing you how to do a resume. Or maybe you didn't even get that: perhaps you've got one of those "career counseling" offices at your school, with services that are available to everyone — and used by no one.

Either way, I think most of you reading this book would probably agree that getting a resume together and actually getting a job are things that are, for the most part, left to you and you alone. But never fear...

I AM HERE TO HELP YOU GET A JOB. That's it. It's the only reason I wrote this book (I guess I wouldn't mind making a few bucks while I'm at it, but I'm not exactly putting J.K. Rowling on notice). I'd much rather help you get a job than stroke your ego. There are already way too many people in the world who would rather kiss your ass, tell you you're awesome, pat you on the back and send you on your way instead of taking a little extra time to help you identify and fix your flaws. You know many of these people already — lots of them are your teachers, friends and parents.

I'm not that guy. Fellas, I'm the stranger who will come up to you and tell you that your zipper is down. Ladies, I'm the guy who will tell you that yes, that dress actually does make you look a little fat. If you think that's "mean," then you're probably not going to like this book. So don't say I didn't warn you.

If you're still here, great — let's get down to brass tacks. The truth of the matter is that most resumes that land on my desk suck, and they suck big time.

Why? Well, the book will go into detail, but let me see if I can sum it up for you. Somewhere around 95% of resumes I see contain varied combinations of: poor spelling, grammar, usage, and mechanics; ugly design; inappropriate information; appropriate information poorly communicated and organized; critical information omitted completely; poor attention to detail, and last but not least, verifiable out-and-out lies.

Chances are, your resume is currently in that 95% screwed-up, toss-it-in-the-trash group, and I'm not just talking to college students or other first-time job seekers. Experienced professionals — this means you as well. Listen up: If you follow the advice of this book, you will move yourself out of the junk pile and into the elite 5% of applicants who are seriously considered for every job they apply for.

And let's talk about those jobs for just one second. I'll go into detail later on in the book, but understand this from the very beginning: Jobs are precious and scarce. The happy days of the past in which you college grads had a guaranteed job waiting for you at the end of the graduation ceremony are long, long gone, and they aren't coming back. The marketplace for jobs is worldwide, and in addition to all your American competition, there are tens of millions of well-educated, hungry (literally, as in, "I need food" hungry) Chinese and Indian workers who are eager to get their first taste of the American Dream. And they are bringing their "A" game with them, and they will be serious challengers for almost any job you may want for — well, for the rest of your working lives.

So, in this new globally hypercompetitive world, will you ever have a legitimate shot at the job you want? Well, that depends. Are you willing to get off your ass and do what you need to do to get it — starting with step one, cleaning up and perfecting your resume? If so, the answer is yes. Excellence, thoroughness and attention to detail is still rewarded, and I believe it always will be. If you'll put the time in, you'll reap the rewards of doing so. But if you're willing to just phone it in and throw a bunch of shit resumes at the wall and see what sticks, then you've probably got a long, grueling career ahead of you that'll be marked by unhappiness and financial struggle.

Here's exactly what I plan to do in this book. I'm going to tell you the truth about the weaknesses in your resume, have you go fix them, and then watch you get a job (and if you're so inclined, you can send me a thank-you letter and I'll tape it to my refrigerator). This book contains a lot of criticism and it focuses relentlessly on what may sometimes seem like small, unimportant details. THEY'RE NOT. THEY ARE WHAT MAKE THE DIFFERENCE BETWEEN HAVING A JOB AND BEING BROKE.

What I'm not going to do is tell you how nice, perfect and wonderful your resume is, and then watch you send it out and get no callbacks. Remember, the time to correct your resumes is NOW, not after you send them out. I wrote this book to stop you from making mistakes that could cost you interviews, so if I'm looking at your resume and find a lot of suggested changes, then that's good. If you're one of the 5% that's doing everything right already, then hey, lucky you, that's even better.

If you can suck up your pride and let me hold your hand on this little journey of self-improvement, you'll immediately skyrocket yourself to the top of your next employer's resume pile, and YOU WILL GET A JOB. (Well, at least you'll get an interview. You might screw that part up, too, but later on in the book I'll help you avoid that as well).

These days, I give seminars to any college that wants to bring me in and have me present the material in this book to its students so they can get jobs. The last lecture I did was at the University of Minnesota-Twin Cities, and the one before that was Harvard University.

OK, that's enough idle chatter. Let's start.

THE FOREST, THE TREES, AND WHATNOT
(OR, "PAINFULLY OBVIOUS THINGS YOU MUST KNOW")

What's the point of a resume, anyway? I mean, if you want the job, why don't you just send a letter and ask nicely if you can have it, pretty please with sugar on top?

That'd be nice — sure would eliminate a lot of time spent polishing and padding a resume. But of course, employers would like to hire someone who can actually do the job, so they ask for a resume.

Well, for some jobs, anyway. In America, we do things a little backward. For lower-paying jobs requiring few specialized skills, we don't ask people to create resumes; instead we use a job application, which usually cuts right to the point. Are you legally old enough to work? Can you work the night shift? Have you ever been convicted of stealing money out of a cash register? How can we get in touch with you? Boom, your Taco Bell application is done, and you're probably being fitted for a drive-thru headset sometime in the next 48 hours.

But strangely enough, as the jobs get more complicated and multifaceted, paying bigger bucks and requiring diverse skill sets and a higher education...we no longer hand out the job applications telling prospects exactly what we want. Instead, we write up a little job description, which almost invariably includes an in-your-dreams description of the "ideal candidate." Something like this:

"The ideal candidate can type 100 words per minute, speaks three languages, demonstrates mastery of all commonly used business software platforms, holds advanced degrees, is generally brilliant enough to do great work but not so brilliant that she will be poached by our competitors or leave to start her own competing business, and is willing to put up with everyone's crap with a smile on her face for an indefinite amount of time while being paid far less than she's worth."

But we don't put all that crap on a job application, because deep down we know that person doesn't exist. Instead, we just invite you to submit your resume.

Shockingly, this doesn't always equal total hiring success; even with resumes to guide them, most employers routinely screw up and hire the wrong person now and then — someone who not only isn't ideal for the job, but someone who absolutely cannot perform the job duties whatsoever. If you think I'm exaggerating, I'm not. This happens, and it happens often. Here's an example of it happening to me. Funny story — funny now, anyway.

Fresh into my first job after graduate school in 1999, I worked at a city-guide website — you know, one of those sites that claims to shepherd you toward the "best of" that particular city, from restaurants to nightlife to shopping, etc. I got a quick promotion over several of my longer-tenured colleagues that led them all to leave the company. Not all at once in some big walkout protest, but close together enough that the manpower exodus left me in a pinch.

I wasn't given the budget to replace them all, but I did get to replace my calendar editor, the person who ensured that all of the sports, music, and other entertainment events going on around town were dutifully entered into our website's calendar. Every time our users found something fun to do, they'd remember they found it at our site, and — we hoped, anyway — become loyal, repeat visitors to our site. It's called "stickiness," and it's very important to people who run websites.

Now, a calendar editor doesn't have to be a Rhodes Scholar; in fact, it's better if she's not. A Rhodes Scholar would get really bored really fast with the tedium that is calendar maintenance. In fact, because it's just repetitive maintenance, perhaps the job should've been called "calendar janitor" or "calendar mechanic;" using the word "editor" conjured up visions of midnight deadlines, last-minute rewrites and gleefully cranking out the scoop of the day, none of which would ever, ever happen to the calendar editor. The job basically consists of entering hundreds of lines into a form, day after day after day. Lather, rinse, repeat. If ever there were a cog in the machinery of Internet media, it is the calendar editor.

And not only did the job require no special knowledge, it also happened to pay extremely well — $35,000. That's not CEO money, but in 1999, for data entry in a cheap city at a cushy office where you can set your own schedule, work with headphones on and drink free Starbucks all day, it was a pretty decent score. (Only during the first-generation Internet bubble could you get paid so much for so little; today most calendar editing is farmed out to virtual assistants in far-flung bastions of $3/hour labor like India and the Philippines.)

Knowing that, it should be very easy to find a good calendar editor, right? Right.

Except it's not.

I had several applicants, all of whom seemed to have a strong pulse and at least 8 working fingers, which is just about all you need in the way of physical prowess to be a calendar editor. But one applicant stood out. Not only could she breathe and chew gum at the same time, but she was actually a former calendar editor for our chief rival website! And at that time, the rival was eating our lunch, so getting their old calendar editor was a giant coup. Not only could she do the job in her sleep, but she'd bring us tips and tricks from the competition that we'd never seen before! We'd have a pipeline to every event in every corner of the Phoenix metro area, from the U2 concerts in the arenas to the back-alley cockfights on the south side. Life was good. Problem solved.

To this day, I don't know what the hell happened with that lady. All I do know is that she showed up and made my life a living hell. I think her name was Brenda, but honestly, I've tried to push all memories of her out of my mind.

She was a nightmare. First of all, she was the slowest computer user I'd ever seen. She'd have 10 events loaded into the calendar when anyone else would've had 50. She spent half the day checking her personal AOL email (it's bad enough that it was personal email, but c'mon, even in 1999, we were laughing at people who were still using AOL). She spent the bulk of the other half on the phone, scolding her lazy teenagers at home for this or that.

She was the first person I ever had to fire, and it sucked. She cried. Sure, I'm a little crass and direct in my writing, but I don't enjoy kicking somebody's world apart in the way that instantly vaporizing their sole income source can do. It was worse because I was barely 25 and she was 40-something, and for whatever reason, that feels extra shitty.

Moral of the story? Simply put, if you have an excellent resume that really stands out above the rest, not only can you get the job you want, but you can even end up swinging a job you're *not qualified for.* Don't get me wrong — we don't want that, and that isn't our goal here. Getting fired sucks.

The goal is to get you the job you want, and a stellar resume is your best ammunition to do that. (Well, other than being a close personal friend of the person doing the hiring, which is always the best scenario. But we'll get to that later).

The Internet has changed everything about the way you'll get your first job — in fact, it's made it a lot more difficult.

How? Because everyone and his mom has access to millions of job listings. Used to be, if you lived in Iowa and saw a job opening, you could be pretty sure that you were only going to be competing with other Iowans for that job. But not today — thanks to the Monster.coms of the world, millions of people from Tokyo to Texas to Timbuktu all have access to that little Iowa job listing.

And that's not all. Your worldwide competitors don't even have to air-mail their resumes across the pond. It's all done in one click of the mouse.

Now, at first, you probably think that's a great thing. From the comfort and privacy of your computer desk, you can apply for 200 jobs around the world in just a couple of hours, right? Sweet!

Well…ok, that's pretty sweet, I'll give you that. But the picture gets dimmer when you realize that, because it's so easy to do, millions of other people are out there doing the same thing. They're applying for the same jobs you're applying for, flooding the employers with thousands and thousands of resumes… and burying yours underneath them all. Each resume that comes in is one that might be better than yours.

So thanks to the Web, every job posted today will get hundreds of applicants, if not thousands.

I'm going to repeat this sentence so many times in this book that I feel like I really ought to be giving a big, splashy introduction. But that's not really my style, so here goes, for the first of what will be many, many times:

Your resume is supposed to be your **supremely rehearsed, error-free, absolute best presentation of yourself,** encapsulated into one piece of paper.

This is the single most important concept of this book, and I repeat it several hundred times (seems like it anyway) throughout the book. This seems obvious, but honestly, most people don't really understand this very simple concept until it's pointed out to them.

Ask someone what their resume is, and the answer goes something like, "it's the thing you send out to get a job." Well yes, but no, not really. It's much more than that, and you can't approach it quite that haphazardly. Here's why:

You, like everyone else in the world, are a complex person with many skills, faults, likes, dislikes, aptitudes, challenges, etc. You could fill a book writing about all the crap you did in the last 12 months alone, but you don't have time to write it. And even if you did, I, your prospective employer, *certainly* wouldn't read it.

Are you kidding me? I'm busy. Really, really busy. I have an entire, 50-hour-a-week job to do, and that doesn't count this whole process of sifting through resumes and doing job interviews. Oh, and I have a family at home who occasionally wants to spend time with me.

So we've established that I don't want to read your life story — at least, not now. But you still want the job, so you have to tell me something about yourself, and it does need to be substantive. Needs to be long on substance and short on B.S.

And this, my friends, is why God created resumes.

Resumes exist for you, the applicant, to succinctly tell me, the employer, everything I need to know about exactly why I should hire you — **and not a bit more**. Later on in this book, I'll examine in some pretty fine detail what you should and shouldn't include in your resume. But first, before you even start your resume (or start to make changes to it, which you'll almost certainly do after you've read this book from beginning to end), here are a couple of things you need to know first.

Many people, especially those applying for their first real job, have a very "wishful-thinking" scenario in their heads about what happens when they send their resumes off to a prospective employer. In this scenario, the boss usually sits at a huge desk in a pristine office with a lovely view. His eyeglasses (or her eyeglasses — you choose, it's your fantasy) are dropped slightly down on his nose, and with every line he reads, he nods ever more approvingly, more assured than ever that you're the best person for the job.

He picks up his phone and calls Smith in the corner office. "Smith, will you getta load of this Jane T. McPickleshitter resume? Wow! Now that's what this company needs around here, a little bitta this McPickleshitter lady!" He hangs up. He hits the speakerphone call button again. "Justin, we need to get this McPickleshitter in for an interview right away. Please call her and set something up this week, today if possible." Justin the Assistant calls you and tells you that Mr. Bossman likes your resume and would like you to come in. You do. After 10 minutes of getting to know each other, your suitability for the throne is confirmed, and the job is yours.

Now, here's what really happens. Your resume arrives in the HR department, where it's opened and placed in a stack with dozens (if not hundreds) of others. The stack continues to grow until the HR department determines it's gotten big enough to pass along — not to the boss, but instead to the Unlucky Slug that gets the job of sorting through them all and culling the best ones down to a manageable handful.

Unlucky Slug probably isn't excited about the prospect of sifting through 800 resumes, since his other job responsibilities haven't decreased any, and this will only pack his schedule more tightly than it's already packed. He's also not getting paid any extra for sifting through them, which, as you might expect, doesn't exactly get him all fired up to roll up his sleeves and dig in.

But he doesn't want to be responsible for hiring a dud, so he does take the task seriously. Over a period of days, he sifts through the stack of resumes, hoping to weed out the 90 that all sound the same, capture the exceptional ones, and then begin the even tougher process of deciding who's the most exceptional of them all.

The stack is huge. You might be at the top of the stack. That's good, because the first ones are always remembered fairly well. You might be at the bottom. That's good, too, because the last ones are obviously the most recent ones Unlucky Slug has seen, and are therefore the freshest and easiest to remember.

But you'll likely be in the middle, and that's not good. People in the middle get forgotten much more often than those at the top or bottom. You probably learned that in Psych 101. Not your fault. It's just how human memory works.

So when that's what you're up against, what do you have to do, what's the solution? Well, obviously you have to make yourself stand out any way you can, and the resume is the place you have to do it.

Remember that I as the employer will never get my first impression from you, yourself. I'll get it from your resume. You may be the most charismatic and knowledgeable person alive. You may have the straightest teeth around, spring-fresh deodorant and a fantastic interview outfit that makes you look so dashing and professional that no one could see you in it without offering you a job, a limo ride home and a $25 gift card to the Olive Garden. But none of that matters if you never get in front of me, and if your resume isn't awesome, you never will.

For this one particular life exercise of finding a job, you have to unlearn all the warm and fuzzy feel-good mantras we were all told growing up. You're one of a kind! There's no one like you in the whole wide world! And my favorite of late, "You are absolutely perfect just the way you are!"

Yeah, sorry — those are all bullshit, and everyone who's ever sifted through a stack of resumes taller than their computer monitor will tell you the same. As diverse as we all are...wow, everyone sure does look extreeeeemely similar when they're condensed onto one piece of paper.

But not to worry. The reason 99% of people look the same on paper is that they have no idea how to differentiate themselves on a resume, and they all put together the same piece of crap they got from their college career office or a pathetic template they got off Google Drive or some freebie website.

After you finish this book, you won't be doing that anymore, and you WILL stand out.

First things first — and this is a lesson you'll use throughout your entire career, so if you're the note-taking type, highlight the following sentence. **If you want to be successful, you have to think less about yourself and more about your audience.** In our case, your audience is Unlucky Slug and Big Boss — the people who are offering money and health insurance and a couple weeks of vacation every year to one lucky winner who is willing and able to come solve problems for them.

Your resume has to please these people, and make them think that you're the best person to come solve those problems.

As an employer, my time is valuable. An employer's mindset is that simply by picking up your resume and looking at it for even 10 seconds, I'm doing you a FAVOR. I don't owe it to you; I don't even know who you are, man, let alone owe you any of my precious time!

This is especially true now, in a situation where there are 100 people applying for every job and internship you post. So before I even lay eyes on it, you, in fact, owe it to me to make the content of this resume worth my time to read it. Everything you include on it should be worth reading. If you waste even one second of my time making me read crap about how you like to paddleboard or brew beer in your garage or dabble in French cooking, I'm going to toss your resume in the trash faster than you can say "I wonder why those guys haven't called me for an interview yet."

Most people screw this up in some way, and I'll talk more about what you should and shouldn't include on your resume later in this book, and we'll make sure you don't do that from this point on. But before we kill this chapter and get on to the meat and potatoes, I give you a warning:

From this point on (ok, and maybe a little before this point), I can start to sound like a super-grouchy asshole that's impossible to please. I urge you to power through it and realize that my hardassery is the strength of the book you're reading right now, not its weakness. If you can buckle down on every detail I give you and turn out a resume that gets an A+ with me, I can assure you that resume is FUCKING BULLETPROOF out in the real world. And that's what you need if you want a job.

Now, on with the show.

GET THE BASIC STRUCTURE IN PLACE.

We'll start simple with the super-basics. There are five basic chunks of information that go into your resume: Header, Experience, Education, Skills and References. In that order (It's not a mistake that I omitted objective. You'll read more about that later).

Header: This is the part with your name and contact information on it. I call it the header because it's usually at the top of the page, unless you're using a more modern design and it's on the side somewhere. You get the gist. At a minimum, include your name, mailing address, best phone number and best email address in this section. If you want to link to your Facebook and LinkedIn pages here (more on that later in the book), that's good too. You don't need much else. Don't worry about a fax number, that's a dying technology.

Experience: This is where you list your past jobs, internships, and basically anywhere else you did work, paid or unpaid (more on that later, too). You'll list the company, your job title, and then bulleted items detailing the specific things you did at the job.

Education: This is where you went/are going to school.

> If you've graduated from college, list the degree and the year you got it (the month or semester isn't necessary) , like so:
>
> *B.A., English, 2014*
> *McPickleshitter State University*
>
> If you're still in college and don't have your degree yet, do the same, with the date you plan to graduate.
>
> *B.A., English, 2016*
> *McPickleshitter State University*

You don't need to put "expected" or "Hopefully!" or anything else by it. If the year you put is in the future, we understand what you mean.

If you have multiple degrees, list them in reverse chronological order.

M.A., Comparative Art Therapy, 2016
University of Palookaville

B.A., English, 2014
McPickleshitter State University

If you didn't attend college but graduated from high school, just list your high school and graduation date.

Diploma, 2008
McPickleshitter East High School

If you didn't graduate from high school but have a GED, do this:

South Dakota High School Equivalency Diploma, 2008
(Doesn't matter if you got an actual diploma)

If you didn't graduate from high school and you don't have a GED, do this:

McPickleshitter East High School, 2004-2007
(If you show a high school and some dates attended, many employers will assume you graduated, even if you didn't. That's cool — let them think so. You didn't lie about it).

Skills: This is where you list all of the skills you have that could conceivably help you do a good job at wherever it is you're trying to get hired. If you're a white-collar type who's going to be at a desk using a computer a lot, list things like the software programs you're good with. If you speak foreign languages, list them here. If you're a construction worker, you might list that you can lay tile, hang drywall, paint, do electrical and plumbing work, roofing, etc.

There are a million job types and thus millions of skills that go along with each, so I can't list examples for everyone. But in addition to those that are job-specific to you, some universal ones are good communication skills, punctuality, conflict-resolution and problem-solving skills. Doesn't matter what job you're applying for, from ditchdigger to CEO — if you always show up on time and you can solve problems creatively, you're a solid prospect.

References: This is where you list the names and contact information for your past bosses, teachers and sometimes co-workers (but never your relatives). There's a whole section on this later on in the book.

Your resume should have all five of these sections. Now, on to more easy stuff...

SPELL EVERYTHING RIGHT. **EVERYTHING.**

Remember that story of the lady I had to fire because she sucked so bad at managing the online events calendar? Yeah, well, a couple years later, I'd moved on from that job and formed my own agency, and, long story short, we got the contract to manage that same events calendar. I left on good terms and still had good connections at the old gig, so my new agency got hired to do it.

Essentially I was in the very same spot as I was a couple years prior, except this time, my company was getting paid to do the calendar editing (instead of a lady who checks AOL all day and cries when getting fired) and I needed to find an actual person to do that instead of me, because I sure as hell didn't want to sit around doing data entry all day.

It was a very important job, but it didn't require a great deal of experience, so we placed an ad at Arizona State University, looking for an intern to handle the job of editing the calendar. We got dozens of responses, but my favorite one went something like this. (Names have been changed to protect those whose permission I didn't ask to include in this book for the purposes of example-making):

Dear Mr. Barsch:

I read with great interest about the job of calender editor with your company. I think I would be an excellent candidate for this job, because I currently work on the events calender for my church, and am very aware of community events and also good with computers. I am excited about the opportunity to become your calender editor and look forward to talking more with you about this opportunity.

Sincerely,
Jane T. McPickleshitter

Maybe I'm biased because I've been a fairly decent speller since I was young, but come on — are you kidding me? The average fifth grader can spell the word "calendar," I guarantee you. And if you can't — hey, get up and walk to one of the walls in your apartment. See that big thing with all the squares and numbers on it? It's a CALENDAR. And because it's a

CALENDAR, I'm certain you can check the cover, and I guarantee you'll see the word "CALENDAR" written somewhere on it. Or, if you're not an analog type, look on your phone. Even $10 drug-dealer prepaids come pre-loaded with a "CALENDAR" app. Copy that spelling. That's all you have to do to get it right.

Against my better judgment, I couldn't resist writing this girl back. I don't consider myself to be a crusader for correct spelling, because that's a losing battle if ever there was one. Usually these things just get deleted, but some people are begging for a little correction. And I told myself to feel good about it, because my "tough love" might actually help this girl someday. So I wrote her back, and my response went something like this:

Dear Ms. McPickleshitter,

Thanks for your inquiry about the calendar job. I wanted to be frank with you and tell you that you were eliminated from consideration for the job due to the fact that you misspelled "calender" three times in your email. To be honest, I couldn't trust you to do error-free work as a calendar editor when you're unable to spell the word "calendar." I wish you the best of luck in the future.

Best regards,
Josh Barsch

I didn't expect her to feel AWESOME when she received it or anything, but sometimes you need to hear the unpleasant truth in order to improve, right? Well, not according to Jane. She actually wrote back.

Dear Mr. Barsch,

I don't know why you had to write me back just to tell me about my spelling. I would have liked it better if you had not written me back at all. I am not a perfect speller, but I still think I could have done a very good job.

Jane T. McPickleshitter

So much for trying to be helpful.

Many people today tend to say that spelling on your resume matters less depending on the nature of the job you're applying for. They say things like, "What do you expect? I'm in marketing!" or "I spray for termites. Don't expect me to win the spelling bee."

But that's not the point. No one expects you to be a perfect speller or grammarian in your day-to-day life; however, your resume is supposed to be your one-time, absolute best possible effort. It's not just you — it's you and the dictionary and the Internet and your aunt who's an English teacher and whoever you can find to proofread it, taking as much time as you need to make this ONE document perfect.

Yes, perfect — no errors whatsoever.

Whether you like it or not, if you misspell words on a resume, you are telling your employer that you're lazy, and that's the worst possible thing to tell a potential employer. We think, "Wow, if this person is putting his/her best foot forward on a resume they only have to put together once and it still looks half-assed, then can you imagine how half-assed his/her work is going to be on a daily basis?"

So how do you get your resume into tip-top, error-free shape, even if you can't spell worth a damn? For starters, of course, use the spell-check function on your computer program. That will catch most of the obvious errors. But once the document is spell-checked, give a copy of it to friends, teachers, spouse, children or whoever else you know that's a better speller than you are. Ask them straight out, "Would you mind taking two minutes to check my resume for mistakes? I'm not a great speller."

Don't be embarrassed to say you're not a good speller — trust me, you're in good company. Once you've had a few people glance over it for errors, you should have an error-free document. It doesn't take long, and it can make the difference between getting the job and getting your resume tossed in the garbage.

I suggest having no fewer than three people other than yourself look over it. If you and three other people look over it and errors still slip through; well, that's just unlucky. And next time, choose three better spellers. Check that: choose five better spellers.

USE CORRECT GRAMMAR.

Most of what I just said about spelling applies to grammar as well, although there is one slight difference: most people, including your potential employers, are not masters of grammar. You can screw up a little here and there, and it'll go unnoticed. For instance, should you say "if I were a rich man" or "if I was a rich man"? Unless you're applying for a copy editor job at a newspaper, it's not a big deal, because copy editors are just about the only people in the world who know every grammatical nuance of the English language (by the way, the answer is "were" — I used to be a copy editor).

On the other hand, if you misspell "calendar," that'll jump out at everyone who sees your resume.

If you don't know the difference between "their" and "there" and "they're" or "its" and "it's" or"your" and "you're," then learn them RIGHT NOW. Here, just this once, I'll help you out:

Their — means it belongs to them. "Have you met Kerry and Ray Barsch? **Their** son wrote a book about resumes, and I'm reading it right now."

There — is somewhere away from here. "If you're looking for that wonderful book Josh Barsch wrote about resumes, it's right **there** on the kitchen table, next to the new-hire packet I just got from the company that just offered me a new awesome job because I listened to his advice."

They're — means "they are." "**They're** already giving me a sweet raise and a promotion at my new job that I got last month, thanks to that killer resume book by Josh Barsch that I bought for a total steal on Amazon for $4.99."

It's — is a short way of saying "it is." "It's a damn shame you don't have a job, and it's probably because you didn't read Josh Barsch's book about resumes."

Its — is how you describe what belongs to "it." "That fine resume book that Josh Barsch wrote, wow... I believe that it's worth **its** weight in gold!"

Your — describes something that belongs to you. "**Your** resume is lovely. How on earth did you make something so lovely? Did Josh Barsch help you with that?"

You're — is a short way of saying "you are." "**You're** a very smart person for buying that book."

Yours — is something that belongs to you. "The job is **yours**!"

Your's — *is not a word. Don't ever fucking type this. Ever.*

LEARNING TO LOVE
THE ONE-PAGE RULE
(OR, FITTING 10 POUNDS OF
SHIT IN A 5-POUND BAG)

As a humor columnist for my college newspaper, The Capaha Arrow at Southeast Missouri State University, I was long-winded and often wrote longer columns than space would allow my editors to print. Hundreds of words had to be cut each time. Seems I loved the sound of my own voice (and if you've gotten this far into this book, I doubt you're surprised).

So my adviser gave me an excellent, if politically incorrect, piece of advice: "The ideal length of an article is the ideal length of a lady's skirt," he said. "Long enough to cover everything, but short enough to make it interesting."

The same holds true for resumes.

If there's one rule that just about everyone has heard about resume writing, it's that you should keep your resume to one page. But is it true? As usual, the answer is, "it depends." If you're a college student — especially an undergraduate student — then 99 percent of the time, the answer is yes, you should keep it to one page.

If you're some kind of wunderkind who was speaking five languages and taking community college classes while your peers were double-dutching and making Pinewood Derby cars, then you may have an argument for a second page. If not, then stick to one page. And I really do mean 99 percent of the time, so this probably means you.

Yes, but: Inevitably, when I talk about the one-page rule, I get at least one or two students who raise their hands and say, "But I've accomplished SO much and I'm in SO many activities and have SO many accomplishments, that I just can't fit all my important information on one page."

My answer? Highly unlikely. Certainly, some students are so busy achieving that, when it comes time to get it all down on paper, it just won't fit. But all that tells you is:

a) You need to be more choosy about what you include in your resume. Your future employer can live without knowing some of this stuff.

b) The things you do include, you need to write about more concisely.

c) You need to use the formatting tools in your word-processing software to your advantage.

Again, I don't say this to discourage you high-achievers out there, or to suggest that you shouldn't be proud of all your accomplishments. You should. I know how you feel. I graduated summa cum laude with a bunch of writing awards and some honor societies and all that.

What I didn't realize at the time, though, was that none of the slave-to-the-grind, real-world employers out there — people who didn't know me from Adam — had the time to recognize and relish every little accomplishment the way my family and friends did. That's just not on their agenda, and it's never going to be.

What IS on their agenda is to find someone to fill the position in front of them. And you can save them time by fitting all of your relevant information onto one beautiful, concise page. Trust me, it can be done.

Keeping your resume to one page will seem difficult at first, but it's not that bad once you learn a few tips and tricks. The tips have to do with the content you do and don't include, and the tricks are in the formatting.

1. Remove the Objective: There, I said it. Whew. I feel better now. There are some things that happen every day in this world that make absolutely no sense, but they keep happening anyway, just because that's the way it's always been. This phenomenon explains, among other things, why The Eagles are still touring, why Taco Bell keeps making new menu items out of the same five ingredients, why they're still making Fast and Furious movies, and so on.

Go ahead and add the resume objective to this list, because if you've never realized how utterly stupid a concept this is, then I'm about to tell you.

I am a psychic. Did you know that? I'll bet you didn't. But I'll prove it, because even though I've never met you or talked to you, I can predict with absolute certainty what your objective is in sending your resume. I promise, I can do it. You ready? Here it comes…

TO GET THE JOB.

Right? That's why you're sending the resume wherever you're sending it — because you want the job — a job, the job, some job, any job.

Now, I have a confession to make: I'm not a psychic, just a smartass. The point here is: the objective is always the same, and everyone knows it: You want the job.

And that's good, because I, the employer, am the one who posted the job. I did that because I wanted to get resumes from people like you who want the job that I posted.

That whole process pretty well goes without saying, right?

Then WHY do people waste a full 20 percent of the space on their one sacred resume page explaining, basically, why they're sending me this resume? I know, I know: the answer is, because somebody, somewhere along the line told you that's what you're supposed to do.

Well, I'm telling you it's not. Go directly to your resume right now, highlight the objective, and cut it out. Now. Seriously, right now, go do it.

You may be afraid to do this. You may think, "but EVERY sample resume I see has an objective, and EVERY book includes an objective section!" Be that as it may, please don't be afraid.

No employer in the history of mankind has ever picked up a resume and said, "Wow, this is a fine resume, except...there's no objective! Maybe they don't really want the job and just sent me the resume to confuse me. Someone's playing a trick on me, because without an objective, I just can't be certain of why this resume ever landed on my desk!"

It does seem ridiculous when you think of it like that, doesn't it?

If you can't bring yourself to remove the objective from your resume — well, I tried. But if you're going to include it anyway, let me give you a piece of advice (sigh, not that you'll probably listen, but I'll give you the benefit of the doubt). Be honest. Say you want the Widget-Maker job that you saw in the paper. Don't attempt one of those fantastically awful snowjobs that go something like this:

"I am seeking a challenging, growth-oriented position where I can develop my communication and organizational abilities and utilize my blah-blah-fucking-blah-whatever skills..."

Ugh. Shut up already. I've read passages in O.J. Simpson's book that are more honest than that.

That's not what you're "seeking" — you're seeking the job I have. Since you sent me your resume, I can only assume you want it, regardless of whether it's challenging or stimulating or gives you goosebumps.

And don't forget, this can backfire on you, too. Maybe I'm ready to offer you a $70,000 job that doesn't have much growth potential. Does that mean I shouldn't call you and give you the job? (Professional Hint: No! Take the job, take the money, learn as much as you can, then jump ship to a better company later.)

2. Remove your GPA: You read that correctly: I said you can leave your GPA off your resume. Slowly back away from this book, breathe deeply, calm yourself down, and when your blood pressure has returned to normal levels, carefully re-approach the book at the next paragraph.

Hey, you're back! Good. Here's the deal about GPA: As far back as you can remember, classroom grades have been the only standard measure of intelligence, so naturally, we've been taught to treat them as important. I won't rant and rave here about how your GPA predicts absolutely nothing about your intelligence, common sense, ability to succeed, etc — but it's true. And even if it was ever a good predictor of anything (which it wasn't), the last 10 years or so have seen a new problem arise: grade inflation.

Grade inflation can be summed up as follows:

At some point in the recent past, someone decided that the horror of seeing the letter "D" or "F" on a report card did much more long-term damage to a kid than, say, not knowing how to read, write or spell. Lots of parents agreed, and convinced schools that even though Johnny still doesn't know what a comma is, he still deserves a B in English.

Consequently, if you want to get a D or an F in 2014, you pretty much have to throw a tomahawk into your algebra teacher's back while he's balancing equations and the chalkboard. Either that, or keep a couple Tylenols in your locker. Then you'll be expelled for sure.

Anyhow, the point is this: Nowadays, just about everyone has a GPA of 3.0 or above. Everyone. So what, you say? Well, it means if everyone has a similar GPA, then **nobody's GPA matters anymore.** That's it, plain and simple — if everyone's GPA is the same (or close), what's the point of even looking?

Yes, but: I can hear it already: "Yes, but today's students are smarter than ever! Classes are more advanced, students are better prepared, and their achievements get more outstanding every day. It makes sense that the GPAs are higher."

It's absolutely true about the students being smarter than ever, the achievements being grander and all that. The stuff that today's top students know and master and achieve is just mind-boggling. Considering the latest generation has been pushed harder than ever — and earlier than ever — by parents to achieve great things, makes it no surprise.

But that just proves the point: if the best students are even better today than before, then why does everyone look the same on paper? If it weren't for the grade inflation phenomenon, the top students would stick out more; but as it is, they simply don't.

Omit your GPA from your resume altogether. I've beaten the grade inflation reason to death already, but it's not the only reason to exclude it. There's also the fact that a high GPA, influenced by grade inflation or not, indicates very little about your suitability for any particular job. That's because the things you have to do to get an "A" in a college class are completely unlike the things you have to do at a job to be successful.

Let's look at this a little more closely, if you don't mind.

Generally speaking, there are three principal tasks you have to perform in any given college class. They are:1) Tests; 2) Papers & Projects and 3) Showing up. Occasionally you'll have a class that gives you extra points for discussion or participation, but for the most part, how well you do each of these three things determines your final grade in any particular class. Now, let's work backward:

Showing up. Did you ever see the movie "Hardball," the inspirational tale of Keanu Reeves teaching love and teamwork to a group of poor inner-city kids? Neither did I, but I caught about 10 seconds of it one day while I was channel-surfing. I caught the part where Keanu, tears in his eyes, tells his ragtag group that "One of the most important things in life is showing up, and I'm blown away by your ability to show up."

I wanted to cry, too, because that's some really dumb advice. It may fly for little children, but in reality, you'll never get a gold star just for showing up. You actually have to do stuff and do it well after you show up in order to be considered a valuable employee. But that's not necessarily true when in college.

More and more professors are making attendance a part of students' grades. Some do it for egotistical reasons — their feelings are hurt when students decide it'd be more interesting to sleep in than to listen to them lecture, so they require attendance. In other cases, parents pressure universities to require attendance, to ensure their hard-earned money isn't paying for classes that their sons and daughters are skipping in favor of watching all-day How I Met Your Mother marathons on TNT (not that I'd know anything about that).

Regardless of the reasons, the outcome is this: you can now get a good chunk of an A just by dragging your ass into class in pajama pants and big fuzzy slippers.

And let's not forget that, in the opposite scenario, lots of college classes don't even count attendance at all, especially at larger schools with class sizes into the hundreds. You can make a total of two appearances all semester — one for the midterm and one for the final — and as long as you can perform well on those two days — that's two days out of 110+ days in a semester — you can get an A.

Obviously, this does not reflect how things really work at a job. You actually have to show up every day and on time, and when you get there, you have to work for about 9 hours straight, with an hour in between for lunch.

Exams. Acing midterms and finals is still the number one way to leave college with an excellent GPA. Exams are supposed to cover the most important concepts and skills that a class has to offer and reveal to what degree you've mastered all these concepts and skills. So why is it that test scores don't necessarily give an accurate forecast of how good you'll be on the job?

There are several reasons, actually. There's an incredible difference in the way "tests" are perceived in college, and in the world outside college. First, let's get clear on what tests are supposed be: a yardstick to measure how much knowledge you have about some given subject at some given point in time. That's pretty much it.

Note that I didn't say it was the final day of reckoning at the Crossroads, the day you must match wits with Satan himself about organic chemistry or Constitutional Law for the right to live the rest of your days above ground. It's just a TEST to see where you are right now. And in the grand scheme of your life and career, "where you are right now" is very near the beginning.

But the college system doesn't treat you that way. It treats you — in every class, at the end of every semester — like you're at the end of the line. Know everything by now, or else. Or else you'll get a bad grade. And because of that, students go about their learning process differently.

Instead of learning as many concepts and skills as they can for the long-term, they do something different: they start preparing for tests.

If you're a college student now or have been a student any time in the last 25 years, you know what I'm talking about. Rarely does a student (and I'm speaking for myself here, too) attempt to read, learn, synthesize and retain all of the material in every course's syllabus. Believe it or not, that's what most of our past generations of college students were expected to do — learn everything the teacher covered in a semester, because you never knew what was going to be on the midterms and finals when they rolled around.

That almost never happens now. Most professors tell you what's going to be covered on the big tests. Many will even review some questions from the actual test with you. Many will hold big review sessions during regular class hours — the class hours you're paying them to teach you new stuff, not old stuff. Some will even GIVE YOU THE DAMNED TEST so you can go home and study it.

That's right — they give you a piece of paper with some questions, you go home and find the answers to those questions, you come back the next period and transfer those answers onto the same piece of paper, and voila — you get an "A" on the test.

Now, many of you are undoubtedly saying, "Yeah….so?" And I probably would've said the same thing when I was in college — whatever freed up my time to meet different girls and drink more Keystone Light (it's not that bad when you get used to it) was fine with me. But my point here is different: it's not to stop partying and start studying all the time — far from it.

The point is, if you're going to study, you might as well be studying something useful that you'll remember, rather than 40 questions on a test that you'll forcefully shove out of your mind once you've dropped the answer sheet on your professor's desk.

There isn't too much professors can do about this — it's simply the way the educational system is set up. The one remedy that's sometimes available is the ability to take a class on the pass-fail system, rather than for a specific letter grade. I have long been a big proponent of pass-fail classes, and still recommend to any student to take a class pass-fail any time you can. But I'll talk more about that later.

Anyhow, as GPA goes, let's boil it down to brass tacks.

What are the possibilities? You have a low GPA — definitely leave it off. You have an average GPA — why include it? What does it add to your application? It's strong — ok, but it's still just GPA, and employers know that the stuff you did to get that GPA is very different from what you'll do at a job. You don't go to work from 9-10 and 2-4 on Mondays, Wednesdays and Fridays and 12-3 on Tuesdays and Thursdays. Work is different.

Possible exception — if you have a really, really high GPA, like summa cum laude high or a 4.0, maybe you should include it. There's still a "wow" factor there, because the likelihood is your boss didn't graduate with that high of a GPA, and it still impresses some people.

That said, remember that most bosses know that your GPA doesn't necessarily mean you'll be a good employee, worker, or anything else.

Yes, but: I've gotten occasional taunts from some students and parents (especially parents) over the years who think I hold GPA in low regard because I never had a very good one myself, and that I'm simply giving you the "I never had a good GPA, and look at me now!" line. Alas, no. I was the salutatorian of my high school class with a 3.96 (we didn't have those highfalutin', five-point AP classes in Box Elder, South Dakota, thank you very much), and I got my B.A. in English with a 3.9. And I promise that's the last you'll hear of me about my own GPA, because it means very little to anyone outside your dinner table. In fact, let me punctuate this point with a final anecdote:

One of the biggest regrets I have about my college education is dropping my French minor. I loved studying foreign languages, and to this day, I still do. (Have you used Duolingo yet? How awesome is Duolingo?) But in the middle of my French III semester, I abruptly dropped the class. Why? I'd had a rough go with a couple of homework assignments and thus I thought I was going to end up with a "B" in the class, and that would hurt my GPA.

Let me be clear here: That decision was **asinine beyond words.** I cannot describe how stupid it was for me to do that. Never once, in the history of my life, has anyone asked me what grade I received in French III. Ever. But because of that choice, there ended my formal French study. There ended my quest to master that beautiful, romantic tongue — to saunter off to Europe and meander through France, Switzerland, Belgium, wooing lovely *francophone* girls into jelly with my rugged American exterior yet oh-so-cultured mastery of le *français*.

But thanks to my absolutely silly pursuit of a few extra hundredths of a point on my undergraduate GPA, my French stinks. I've been to Montreal and Paris and stammered like a fool each time, relying only upon the locals' goodwill toward English-speakers to get by (lots more of that goodwill in Montreal than Paris, by the way).

Oh, well. I was only in Paris for my honeymoon anyway, so I guess my wife would've put a stop to any lovely-French-girl wooing even if I could've managed some. But still.

Don't be like me. Learn what you want to learn and forget about the GPA. You will never, ever regret it.

3. Remove your wealth of personal activities: If you like to water ski, or play shuffleboard or crochet dog sweaters, good for you. As an employer, I don't give a shit. If this resume is truly your one-time, one-page, rehearsed best effort, then your personal interests don't belong anywhere on it. If the value you could bring me and my company is so sparse that it doesn't fill one measly page, and to fill out that page you're forced to bring up the fact that you like jet skis and golf and that you're a foodie and a huge Vikings fan, then you don't bring enough to the table to merit serious consideration.

Yes, but: But aren't your personal interests an expression of your "real self" — the person behind the paper, the human being that these people would be interacting with every day if they were to hire you? Yes indeed, and that's another reason to OMIT the personal information, regardless of how wonderful a guy/gal you think you are (and may very well be).

Here's what you may not be realizing: On a personal level, your boss may be a complete jerk (this has been known to be the case — just ask anyone who's ever had a job). He may like what you hate and hate what you like. He may annoy you, and you may annoy him. Your love of reality TV may lead him to think you're a nitwit. Your passion for three-wheelers may bring to mind those little bastards who ride their Razor scooters up and down his street at night, robbing him of the sleep he desperately needs to make him less of an asshole in regular daily life.

So why risk bringing up such irrelevant things in the first place? After all — and this is the most important part — no one who needs help on the job badly enough to necessitate hiring someone is going to hire you based on the things you do outside of work. It's what you can do for your boss on the job that will get you hired.

After reading the previous pages, you may think I'm a complete stiff who's totally against having fun at work. Nothing could be further from the truth; in fact, I've always made my job as much fun as I possibly could and encouraged everyone around me to loosen up and do the same. But I do that after I've already gotten the job.

There's a time and place for your personality to come out. That time is after you're hired, and that place is the water cooler, lunches, meetings, etc. Once the papers are signed and you've got a paycheck, that's the time to get to know the people in your office. You won't like everyone, and everyone probably won't like you, either.

But that's fine if you've already got the job — working with people you don't like is as inevitable as death itself. You just don't want them ganging up on you beforehand and convincing the boss that you aren't worth hiring in the first place.

4. Omit fraternities and sororities. Everything I said about personal interests also goes for social Greek organizations, and also most service fraternities.

Yes, but: Aren't fraternities and sororities great for networking after college is over — including job-market networking? Yes, they're definitely great for networking. And I must confess that I never joined a fraternity, so I don't have personal knowledge of exactly how far a frat-brother connection will go in the way of landing you a job.

My conversations with Greek friends and acquaintances, however, indicate that such a connection is sometimes more than enough to get your foot in the proverbial door. In light of that, I might make one exception to the above rule: If you're applying for a job where you know that one of your fraternity/sorority members works and has hiring discretion, then you may want to sneak your affiliation onto your resume.

Again, I emphasize this approach only for jobs where one of your Greek brethren has some pull. Otherwise, in a normal job-opening situation where you're going in cold, fraternity and sorority membership won't impress the person reading your resume.

Yes, but (Part II): "Greeks do lots of charity work, so my association with a fraternity or sorority is relevant for that reason."

It's true that Greeks do a lot of charity work, but charity work is not the reason for their existence. So you can't claim a "halo entry" on your resume (that's what I call a resume item that's only there to make you look like an angel) for a fraternity the way you could for, say, working at Habitat for Humanity.

Most of your employers have been to college, and whether we were Greek or not, we know that the primary reason a person joins a fraternity or sorority isn't to do charity work. There's plenty of charity work out there that doesn't require pledging, hazing, and dues. And that's not a knock on Greek life at all — to each his own — but let's call a spade a spade.

5. Omit high school stuff: Almost without exception, you should not put high school achievements on your resume. Unless you're Jack Andraka (the kid who invented a super-cheap and super-sensitive early-detection test for prostate cancer at age 14) or you saved the world from certain destruction and have the newspaper articles (remember newspapers?) to prove it, leave this stuff out.

Why? Because things were different in high school. You were competing against a hodgepodge of 16- and 17-year-olds thrown together by geographic convenience. Many of those teenagers had no interest whatsoever in competing with you for grades, awards, honors, etc. Some others dropped out altogether to (pick one) join a gang, deliver pizza full time, follow ICP around the country, or smoke cigarettes at the mall. (If your town still actually has a mall, that is. You probably can't smoke cigarettes in it anymore, though. Well, given the state of malls these days, you can probably smoke anything you want in there and get away with it, actually.)

The fact that your accomplishments bested those of your above-mentioned peers five years ago is not impressive to a present-day employer. It's not that you can't still feel good about it. Hey, I still treasure my high-school discus medals and that time I took third out of 150 competitors in an English Literature competition. But I don't put it on my resume, because no one who sees my resume would care. Actually, no living person on Earth would care. Not even my mom.

The reason you don't include that stuff is that you're into a much higher level of competition now. Everyone you're competing with wants exactly the same thing you want: the open job. And there aren't any slouches competing with you anymore — those guys smoking cigarettes at the mall (yes, they're still there) are not the ones competing with you now. Everyone you're up against has a similar background, education and skill set. Because of that, it's important that you emphasize your recent accomplishments — ones that you've carved out for yourself against your current crop of competitors, rather than people from the past who weren't really breaking their necks to compete with you in the first place.

Yes, but: "What about major accomplishments, like becoming an Eagle Scout?" There are indeed some accomplishments that mark a person for life, and garner praise for many years — even decades — after they're earned, even if they're earned during a person's high school years. In this case, I'd make an exception to the above rules and include the accomplishment on your resume. For example, there's no way I'd leave "Eagle Scout" off my resume, especially since I dropped out of Cub Scouts the first time they asked me to tie a complicated knot. Knots are hard.

There may be other awards that carry similar weight, but I'm not aware of them, so your decision whether to include such an award in your resume will be up to you. But before you take the natural step of assuming your award or accomplishment is prestigious enough to include, ask yourself one question: When you tell people who don't know you about your award, do they have to ask you to explain what that is? Or is it an accomplishment, like Eagle Scout, that everyone instantly recognizes? If it's the former, then it probably doesn't belong on your real-world, job-market resume.

EDUCATION VS. EXPERIENCE
(OR, "WHAT ALMOST EVERYONE GETS WRONG")

One of the most common mistakes I see among college graduates — along with using an objective — is listing the education section of your resume above the experience section. I don't know where it all started, but somewhere along the line, everybody started doing it, and it got passed down the line. It's terrible advice, and here's why.

With apologies to the blue-bloods out there whose Mommies and Daddies secured their future employment before they emerged from the womb (and why would any of them be reading this book anyway?), here's a fact that everyone else has to realize: Experience counts for not just a lot, but one hell of a lot more than education. Not only that, but a good education is simply the closest acceptable substitute for people who have no experience whatsoever.

Put another way, where you went to school and how you did while you were there tells me how well you MIGHT be able to do if you were offered the chance to GET some experience (namely, in the open position that I've advertised). But if someone out there has experience already, then I'm likely to spend much less time training that person to do what I need to have done than I'd spend on the person with a nice education but not a lick of experience.

Education is a commodity. The word "commodity" is misused all the time in the everyday vernacular. Quick, what's the most common usage of the word that pops into your head? That's right — when someone is referred to as a "hot commodity," which means that they're very in demand or popular at the moment.

But that's not what "commodity" actually means. It's the opposite, actually — a commodity is something that's essentially the same as everything else like it. It's indistinguishable from and interchangeable from other things like it. That's why "hot commodity" is a misnomer — if you're a "commodity," you ain't hot.

Ever hear the talking heads on CNBC or Bloomberg financial shows talking about the "commodities market"? They're talking about stuff like coffee beans, wheat, corn, etc. We call these things commodities, which means there isn't much difference between coffee beans in Africa or Jamaica or Guatemala. Sure, there are subtle variations in quality and flavor, but at end of the day, a bean is a bean is a bean. It's not like the difference between a Ferrari and a Ford Fiesta. *(Organic gardeners, please do not write me nasty emails based upon the above paragraph; you get the gist of what I mean.)*

So, where does your education fit into all this? Is a college education simply a commodity, the same everywhere?

Well, yes and no. It's what you make of it. What you decide to learn and master while you're in college determines whether your education is a Ferrari or a Ford Tempo. But in terms of the way you represent that education on a resume, it's pretty much all the same. Everyone applying for your job probably has an education of some sort, and your resume entry probably looks like this:

BACHELOR OF WHATEVER

Wherever State University, 2002

As you might guess, there isn't a lot of difference between these entries: only the names, places and dates change. And as we discussed earlier in this book, when everything looks the same, it starts to mean less and less, and your prospective employers just tune out the entry altogether.

Here's the deal about the education section of your resume: In most cases, it's hastily scanned at best, and even then, it's just to make sure that you actually have an education of some kind. Very rarely will anyone assign massive value to the school you came from; at the same time, it's just as rare that you'll be overlooked because you went to a smaller or lesser-known college.

Let me repeat that for the millions of parents out there who have children wanting you to spend an extra $175,000 on a "name-brand" school. **You will not be overlooked for a job because you didn't go to a marquee school.** Some of the greatest people I've ever worked with came straight from community colleges, and some of the most useless came from the Ivy League. Trust me — your future boss will not run to check your school's ranking in the *U.S News & World Report* college rankings to help her decide whether you'll be a useful employee.

On the other hand, let's look at experience. The variety of different people's experiences is absolutely unlimited. Each job has a different title and is performed at a different company and has different responsibilities and tasks that must be carried out every day.

Two candidates who have exactly the same Bachelor's of Whatever from the University of Wherever may have vastly different levels of experience. One may have done little more than make coffee and sort mail at her internship, while the other may have taken on a great number of critical responsibilities at his. As you may have guessed, we employers tend to give much greater weight and respect to the latter.

Yes, but: I can already hear you now — "But I don't have any experience! I'm looking for my first job here, man! I got nothin'!"

I hear this all the time, and fortunately, it's bullshit every time! Of course you have experience — you just don't realize it. Everyone has experience of some sort. Have you lived in a cave for the last 20 years? If not, then you have experience. Here are some examples:

Internships. For students who are still in college, internships are the most popular form of experience on a resume. There's a good reason for that: just about every business out there loves interns. Adores them.

We love interns because you're cheap! And a lot of the time you're absolutely free. And it's not the type of free labor you get from prison chain gangs or DWI convicts doing community service work. You actually want to be there, you're smart, you've got some preexisting knowledge about the business, you're busting your hump to prove you're worthy, and oh, by the way, you work for less than the guy who cleans the bathrooms. What's not to like?

Because of this, internships abound, and probably always will. Which brings me to my next point: don't rely on your department office, or your career counselors, or even the Web, to give you a listing of all internships out there, because they can't. They'll give you the high-profile and long-established ones, but that's it.

It's very, very easy to not just find little-known internships, but to create them yourself. Your ability to do this depends on your willingness to take a pauper's wages for your work, but that's pretty much status quo for most internships you'll find. Here's how you do it:

Decide where you want to do an internship. Look around the company's website for the highest-ranking person in the department you want to work for. (If the company's small and doesn't have a website, call and ask for the owner or general manager. When he/she gets on the phone, ask their name. Then hang up. Now you know!)

Next, go to the company's office — physically, take yourself down to the office (and bring your resume). Ask for the person whose name you've just discovered in the previous paragraph. When they emerge, tell them briefly who you are, and that you'd like to give them your resume. Introduce yourself like this:

"I'm Jane T. McPickleshitter, and I'm a student at Wherever State

University. I'd love to do an internship here, and I'm willing to work for minimum wage helping you out in any way you need me to help out."

Do that, and you've got a 50-50 shot. Your chances increase greatly by modifying the approach to:

"I'm Jane T. McPickleshitter, and I'm a student at Wherever State University. I'd love to do an internship here, and I'm willing to work for free, just to gain the experience and a resume entry, helping you out in any way you need me to help out."

No matter how presumptuous it may be to simply barge into someone's office and hand them your resume, the prospect of competent free labor is an aphrodisiac that very few businesspeople can resist. Add to it the fact that you're obviously a bold and enthusiastic volunteer, and your chances of getting work go through the roof.

Of course, I understand that some people have bills to pay and can't devote a great deal of time to volunteering. But remember — an internship that takes 5-10 hours a week fills up space on a resume just the same as one that takes 35-40 hours a week. If you can trim back your activities just a bit here and there, maybe you can make it work.

I've had at least a dozen students tell me, "Well, yeah, I did an internship, but it was unpaid, so I couldn't put it on my resume."

Uh...are you nuts? Of course you put it on your resume! Did you learn any less because you weren't paid? Did you do any less? Of course not. Paid or unpaid makes no difference at all on your resume. What matters is that you worked and learned somewhere. And no, you need not designate "paid" or "unpaid" in parentheses after you list the internship on your resume.

Yes, that includes volunteer jobs. Of course it does!

- If you're the volunteer treasurer for a local dog-rescue operation, then guess what? That's still a job managing the finances for a nonprofit organization, and it definitely belongs on your resume.
- If you're a plumber who fixes stuff for free at a children's home... you're still fixing stuff and doing the work. Put it on your resume!

"Unrelated" job experience is not always as unrelated as you think.

One bit of bad (although well-meaning) advice I often hear is to exclude work experience that's "unrelated" to the job you're seeking. Sometimes that's true, but often it's not.

Reason 1: Sometimes you're incorrect in assuming it's unrelated. Would you put Burger King experience down on a resume if you're applying for an accountant job? Consider this example:

Let's say you're trying to get the aforementioned accounting job, and four years ago you were an assistant manager at Burger King. You worked the closing shift at BK, during which you'd tally up the books every night — labor costs, revenue, bank deposits, all that. Should you include this on your resume for an accounting job? HELL YES, you should! You were in charge of the financials every day at a successful store in a national mega-franchise. There is no question it should be on your resume.

Reason 2: Even if the nature of the work is truly unrelated, it can still be valuable information to your potential employer. Let's say you made Whoppers and Croissan'wiches at Burger King 35 hours a week for three years while you were in college studying to be an architect. That's impressive for the work ethic alone, man. I worked my ass off at Dairy Queen, Taco John's and McDonald's for years, and the work sucks. It takes a strong work ethic to do that kind of work week in and week out when you could probably just kick back and survive on student-loan money. I never begrudge anyone for putting fast-food or other related drudgery on their resumes. It shows me they're willing to bust ass and work hard when they need to.

MAKE DIFFERENT RESUMES FOR DIFFERENT JOBS
(OR, "ONE SIZE DOES NOT FIT ALL")

In all but the rarest of cases, people are qualified to do — or at least minimally capable of doing — several different jobs. And honestly, if you think you're one of the rare few out there who can only do one specific thing for pay — you probably just aren't desperate enough yet. You'd be surprised what capabilities you discover when the rent is due and you've only got $17 in your checking account.

As I sit writing this paragraph in the summer of 2014, the job market is mediocre. Nowhere near the worst I've ever seen (that would be right after the 9-11 bombings), but a far cry away from the best (that would be during the first Internet bubble in the late 1990s, where anyone with a pulse and basic computer literacy could have a $55,000 job with free Starbucks all day and unlimited ping-pong privileges in the break room. God I miss those days.).

My point is, for those of you who are not in some ridiculously high-demand field with more openings than there are people to fill them, you'll probably find yourself applying for a variety of different types of jobs. In that case, you will want a separate resume for each type of job.

You want to appear as if every job you're applying for is a perfect match for you and your skill set. This, of course, is bullshit — few jobs you apply for in your life will be the ideal mix of your strongest skills and wildest occupational desires — but that's OK. Everyone does this kind of bullshitting, and employers don't even mind it — we know you're doing it, too. We've done it ourselves.

Sometimes you just need a job, man. We get it. But you still have to sell yourself to us with the best pitch you can muster up, and that usually involves pretending to be way more excited and qualified than you actually are. You can't really go in with a resume that says, "Well, this is miles away from anything I'd prefer to be doing and I certainly don't foresee enjoying myself here, but I can probably do a half-ass decent job until either you find somebody better or I find another opening at a different company that sounds more interesting to me, after which I'll disappear in a puff of smoke."

Even sympathetic employers won't hire you then.

So, let's say you've got at least entry-level competency in graphic design for print, web design, public relations, and advertising sales. In this scenario, you'll need a print design resume, a web design resume, a PR resume and an ad sales resume.

For these field-specific resumes, you want to take all your experience, skills and training in that specific area and make it the most prominent content in your resume. Essentially, in this example, your print design resume should contain entirely print design-related skills and experience; your ad sales resume should contain entirely ad sales-related experience and skills, etc.

Let's take the print design resume as an example.

Any print-design jobs or internships should come first on your resume. Even if you've had a single task at a job that otherwise had nothing to do with graphic design — say, you worked at McDonald's, but between drive-thru shifts you were asked to design the employee newsletter — that belongs in your print-design resume as well.

Because this resume is specific to one particular type of job, you can leave other, unrelated things out — let's say, in keeping with our example here, your public relations and ad sales experience and skills — and that leaves you more space to talk about other graphic-design related stuff that you've done. In your previous, one-size-fits-all resume, you didn't have a lot of extra space to work with, given the fact that you were trying to cram every bit of your skills and knowledge into one page.

Now you can enter more details about your graphic design projects, skills and expertise. For example, instead of one entry listing all the software you've mastered, you can go into greater detail about what you can do with image-editing software, illustration software, video-editing software, etc.

The big benefits of creating job-specific resumes are:

a) You eliminate a lot of admirable but mostly irrelevant information from your r esume, because in most cases, nobody cares if a graphic designer can sell ads, or if an ad salesperson can use Photoshop, etc. Don't get me wrong; it is, in fact, a good thing to have someone on your staff who knows multiple areas of the business, because that means they likely understand the company better. However, that type of well-roundedness isn't going to trump deep, extensive knowledge and skill that are key to the specific job being advertised here. If a graphic design job is at stake, a tremendously skilled graphic designer who couldn't sell ads to save her life is going to get the job over a merely competent designer who could sell ads in a pinch.

b) Because you've eliminated that less-relevant info, you get to replace it with stuff that matters to the open position at hand. Now your resume has double the relevant info, and you're twice as attractive a candidate as you were before. Nice work!

INCLUDE A PHOTO WITH YOUR RESUME
(OR, "PAINFULLY OBVIOUS THINGS YOU MUST KNOW")

When I was a graduate student at the University of Missouri, few topics of discussion generated the ferocity of debate as the question of whether you should attach a photo to your resume. For most readers, this is a completely new idea. It's rarely mentioned in any books on the subject, and ten bucks says you've never had a career counselor mention it to you.

For me, there's no debate at all: you should definitely attach a photo if you've got a nice one, and if you don't have a nice one, go get a nice one and attach it. But I'll present both sides of the argument below, though I make no promises about shielding you from my bias. Because I'm right and the other side is wrong.

First, let's set some parameters. When I say "photo," I mean a professionally done headshot. Not a Polaroid, not a snapshot of you on vacation, not a candid of you in a suit at your cousin's wedding cropped from the neck up, and certainly not you in clubwear with bloodshot boozy eyes and one of your bro's arms wrapped around your neck while the other is fist-pumping.

I'm talking about a professional headshot that you can get done for about $39 from any photographer in your town. If you're a man, you wear a jacket and tie in the photo. If you don't have a jacket and tie, borrow one from someone you know for an hour while you get the picture taken (then go buy one, because eventually you'll need one). If you're a woman, wear a "smart business suit," as the magazines call it. If you don't have one, borrow one, or go buy one and return it the next day after you get your photo taken.

Why would you attach a photo to your resume, anyway? For one, it's simply a good way for the employer to put a face with a name. When there's a stack of 100 resumes on your desk, it's hell trying to remember who's who and what's what. If you include a photo, you're doing me a massive favor; all of a sudden, you're "the one with the photo." You immediately stand out. Immediately. I cannot emphasize this enough.

Another reason is a simple fact of life: Appearance counts; in fact, it counts a lot. That doesn't mean you have to be an Adonis or a beauty queen to get a job. Let's face it, if it did, our unemployment rate would be MUCH higher than it is.

No, it just means you have to tend to your appearance when you're trying to get a job, even if you rarely do at any other time. If you look good, clean and well-groomed, then you've automatically made a good first impression in that area. Again, this isn't about beauty; it's about hygiene and presentability (I'll go into the specifics later in the section about job interviews). And from an employer's perspective, there's something nice about knowing what the person's going to look like when he/she walks through the door for the interview.

WARNING! POLITICALLY INCORRECT
SUBJECT MATTER AHEAD!

You can't address this subject completely and honestly without addressing two subjects that inspire a lot of heated opinion: discrimination and physical attractiveness. Let's start with the lighter of the two, physical attractiveness.

In this photo-or-no-photo debate, someone always mentions that attractive men & women use photos to gain an advantage that's unmerited, and that doing so debases the job itself by attempting to artificially inject sex appeal into the job criteria. This argument always reminds me of a survey that's released every so often about what regular people would do in certain ethical situations. The following question or a similar one always seems to come up:

> *You're offered a job that you really want. You have yet to accept the job when you're told that part of the reason you were hired is because of your physical attractiveness. Do you still take the job?*

Most people say yes. It's a rare person who turns down a job because someone thought they were hot. In fact, if you're a guy or a girl who's commonly considered sexy by the people you run into, it's doubtful this is the first time you've been on the fortunate side of preferential treatment due to your good looks.

How would you answer that question? Never mind, I don't really care. The point is, if you're like a majority of job-seekers, you don't care if your looks work to your advantage from time to time, so the fact that this might occur probably shouldn't deter you from including a photo of yourself when you send out your resume.

Yes, but is it *fair*? Honestly, questions of "fairness" like these are of almost no interest to me whatsoever. One of the first things I can remember learning from my parents is that life isn't fair. They were right, and everyone knows it.

Is it fair that tall men are promoted to executive positions at a far higher rate than short men are? Of course it's not. But it still happens, and that really stinks if you're a short guy. At the same time, you don't find many tall men sawing off their legs at the knee just to level the playing field, do you?

The playing field isn't completely level — never has been, never will be. Princes are embraced more often than frogs. That's just how it goes.

I say, it's better to confront this slanted playing field up front, and you do that with a photo. If I'm going to lose out on a job to an equally competent woman whose sexy legs send my prospective employer into swoons of fantasy, then that's life — and I'd rather know it up front. The alternative is for me to fly halfway across the country to interview the job, rent a hotel, rent a car, do a fruitless interview, fly back home — and STILL lose the job to my sexy peer.

Think about it — if the person making hiring decisions will discard your resume based on your photo, do you really think he/she wouldn't do the same after seeing your mug in person? We're talking about people here who are either racist and or sexist, and enough so that those beliefs will drive their hiring process. A 30-minute interview with you isn't gonna change any of that, no matter how dazzling you are.

This is a good time to re-state the sole goal of this book, which is **to help you get a job**. Period. To that end, my position is that if you think it'll help you get the job, do it. And attaching a photo undoubtedly does the following: a) helps you stand out from the resume stack; b) helps you send additional information to your employer that a resume doesn't (i.e., "I clean up nice and project a professional image"); and c) It accelerates the process by which a racist or chauvinist employer will eliminate you from consideration if something about you doesn't meet his/her off-the-books, non-merit-related criteria. Yes, item C doesn't help you get a job exactly, but it does speed up the process of eliminating you from a job you don't have a chance of getting, and pushes you forward to the next job that you've got a better chance at.

Speaking of racism and sexism, our two other elephants in the room:

Back in grad school, a frequent point of debate was whether sending a photo attached to a resume enabled a level of pre-screening by bigoted employers. The argument here was pretty simple: if you're a woman or an ethnic minority (essentially anything other than a white guy), it encourages others to pre-filter you out based on racial or gender bias.

I actually agree with that. Of course it does. If someone doesn't want to hire a black guy or a Hispanic woman or an Asian transgender woman, a photo certainly helps them make that decision quickly and easily.

The core of the debate really lies in the question of whether the minds of those people who would discriminate against a person can/will be changed if they discover their applicant is black/female/Hispanic/transgender or whatever later on in the process. Personally, I think that if someone has decided they're not going to hire you because you're black or a woman or Hispanic, then they're not going to hire you when you show up in person, either.

Others believe that yes, if you show up as a brilliant candidate and ace the interview and knock their socks off, you'll get the job anyway. I do see merit in this position, especially when hiring is done by committee, as it often is. If a minority candidate comes in and blows everyone away in the interview, it's considerably harder for the lone bigot to exert his/her negative influence over the entire hiring group.

But I still advise you to send a photo, because I think it does way more good than harm in most cases. And my advice is the same regardless of your race, gender or sexual preference. I'm a white guy so I'll admit my bias here, but I strongly believe in putting yourself out there, exactly as you are. Be proud and confident, whoever and whatever you are.

Then get a nice picture taken of yourself looking proud and confident and attach it to your resume.

POLISH PROTECT
YOUR DOCUMENTS
(OR," THE 99-CENT SUIT
OF ARMOR NO ONE USES")

Do you have a resume handy? If so, grab it. Look at it. It may be in pristine shape now, but it's awfully delicate and easy to tear up, dog-ear, spill your breakfast on, etc.

Let's avoid that. Instead, let's construct a scenario where your prospective employer is, consciously or subconsciously, delighted with the presentation of your resume.

Use a slick folder with slits for business cards. There are multiple elements to this tip, so let me break them down one by one.

First, the folder itself. ALWAYS send your resume in a folder; don't ever just slide the paper into an envelope and send it on its way to be terrorized, battered and abused by the postal system. By the time it finally lands in your employer's lap, it'll be dog-eared and wrinkled at the very least.

Yes, this means you'll have to buy a lot of folders, and not the cheap-o kind (more on that later). But trust me, these little steps add up to a very big difference in the way your resume is perceived *before anyone even bothers to read it.* If you've gone to the trouble to preserve the professional appearance of your resume, it demonstrates that you're detail-oriented and you care about the way things look. Better yet, it demonstrates what you're not, which is careless and lazy.

Second, the "slick" part: Among the numerous folder choices at Office Max (or wherever you buy office supplies) should be some glossy black or navy folders. These are my personal favorites, and they're what I recommend you use to send your resume to prospective employers. Don't get the shitty 4-for-$1 kind everyone snatches up at Wal-Mart during back-to-school sales. Get the expensive kind.

There's another intangible involved in these folders, and it doesn't make a lot of rational sense, I'll admit, but I still believe it's true. When an employer gets a resume in a very nice, high-quality folder, I've found that a) he doesn't like to separate the resume from the folder, which means that, if you're lucky enough to make the cut and have your resume passed around to other decision-makers in the company, it'll be passed around in that nice folder, which is a plus, since it looks so damned nice, and b) he doesn't like the idea of getting rid of that folder. I mean, hey, it's not a 19-cent Kmart special — it's a fine, slick-looking folder. Who wants to trash that?

Rationally, of course, this makes no sense. The folder probably cost 99 cents down at Staples. There is no reason under the sun for an employer to be captivated and emotionally attached to any item that costs 99 cents. But many are. I can't say why, exactly, but perhaps it's because that's 99 cents more than almost every other job applicant cared to spend in order to make a good impression with you.

Now, the part about the slits for the business cards. If you've never seen folders that have these, they look like any other folder from the outside, but on one of the inside flaps, they have four small slits that are designed for the four corners of your business cards (if you don't have business cards yet, we'll address that in a second). You may have to look a little harder for these, but not too hard — they're available at all office-supply stores.

Get business cards made, and insert them into these slits. "Business cards for what?" you're wondering. "I don't even have a job yet!"

That's true. But you still have a name, address, contact information and skills — all of which you can advertise to your prospective employers on a business card that they can slip into their pocket, stash in their contact file, etc. And not only that, but yes, you even have a position, even if it's not the official position given to your employer-to-be.

Just because you don't have a job doesn't mean you're nothing — it just means you don't have a job. Therefore, regardless of whether you're employed at the moment, on your business card you can still be a Broadcast Journalist, a Marketing Professional, a Software Engineer, an Interior Designer, a Sous Chef, or whatever it is that you're good at and plan to do with your working life.

A name, contact info, and a job title — that's all you need to make a business card. And by the way, business cards are extremely cheap nowadays, especially when you order them on the Internet. Surely you've heard of VistaPrint, right? They're even free sometimes, but the free ones usually have the printing company's name and URL emblazoned on them somewhere, which I don't recommend. Spring an extra $10 or so and get them without VistaPrint's watermark.

> OK. Let's summarize our efforts here and examine the difference they make in the eyes of your prospective employer.

> Almost everyone else has sent their resume as a piece of paper inside an envelope. Some have actually folded it into thirds so it'll fit into a standard-sized envelope, so it'll have lovely crease marks all over it. Some will step it up a tiny bit and send a full-sized envelope that doesn't require folding. Yay for them.

> When your package arrives, it's on an entirely different level. What the employer pulls out of the envelope is a slick, heavy folder. Inside is your resume, in pristine condition. Accompanying it is a business card, also in pristine condition.

> Immediately you have elevated status among the stack of resumes — at the very least on a subconscious level, but quite often on a very conscious and acknowledged level. "Wow. This is really nice. This person has their shit together and obviously takes this seriously. Christ, they even have business cards."

I assure you that many variations of those statements will follow the unveiling of your resume nearly every place you send it.

Does that mean you're a cinch to get the job? Of course not. It's a dog-eat-dog world out there and there's still plenty of tough competition. But this is about giving yourself *every possible advantage*, and going the extra mile to give yourself a slick, polished and professional presentation from the moment the employer opens your envelope is an excellent way to do that.

"REFERENCES
AVAILABLE
UPON REQUEST"
(OR, HOW TO NEEDLESSLY PISS ME
OFF, MAKE MY JOB HARDER AND
ANNOUNCE HOW LAZY YOU ARE)

"References available upon request." We've all seen it. It used to be on my own resume long ago, actually, and chances are damn good it's on yours right now.

We're about to fix that. You're welcome in advance.

This insane, legacy practice runs neck-and-neck with the Objective as the most annoying, ubiquitous, aggravating inclusion on resumes today, both for new as well as experienced job-seekers.

Why is it such a big deal? First let's recall some important things that we've already learned: You're competing with hundreds of other people for this job, and the employer already has a stack of resumes on her desk that's taller than she is. She's very busy, OK?

So along come you and your resume. You've read the first part of this book and listened up good, so after 95 percent of the resumes met Mr. Paper Shredder, you're still in the running. Good for you!

And so the boss lady is reading over the finalists. Your resume looks sharp.

Great achievements, all meat and no fat. A cornucopia of marketable skills. Impeccable spelling and grammar. Her eyes continue down the paper to find a bold-faced header titled **References.** "Excellent," she thinks. "This Jane T. McPickleshitter is a sharp candidate. I'm glad she saw fit to include some references, because an endorsement from a former boss or two is just about all I need to make my decision."

And then she sees you've tricked her. It's a prank. You've literally gone and pranked the person who is just about to decide to very possibly give you a few hundred thousand dollars over the coming years.

You added a **References** header…but you were kidding. There are no references here — instead, there's that detestable line of text that says, "Available on request."

Let me tell you why this is an incredibly stupid thing to do.

- Everyone has references "available upon request." I know perfectly well that I can call you and ask for references if I feel like it. You did not enlighten me by telling me that I could do so. Why did you decide to fuck with me and slap a "References" heading on your resume and then pull the rug out from under me?

- In a competitive job landscape — and believe me, from now until you die, every job landscape is going to be competitive — it's breathtakingly arrogant to assume that there's any possibility under the sun I wouldn't want some references. It's like saying, "On the off-chance that you haven't literally shit your pants in astonishment at what a dazzling job candidate I am, head and shoulders above every other person who applied for this job, and you aren't ready to just hire me on the spot, sight unseen, without ever having spoken a word to me…then (HUGE SIGH…) I guess I can pull together some names and numbers for you to call. But really, who are we kidding? I'd like to start next Monday. Please have a strong cup of black coffee on my desk and an unmarried, promiscuous secretary waiting in my office."

Not fucking likely. *Of course* we want to see some references.

Now, that doesn't necessarily mean we'll actually call them all — maybe so, maybe not. Depends on how busy we really are. But they'll definitely be scanned, and we'll take note of who you put down and make some kind of subconscious snap judgment. Did you put down high-level people at previous jobs? Did you put down your mom and brother? Whether we call them or not, we'll take a look, then process and judge you by the people you chose to include.

But if you didn't even bother to include any in order to give us the opportunity — then you'll end up in the garbage.

(P.S.: Don't put your mom down as a reference. That's actually worse than saying "Available Upon Request".)

I may have mentioned this once or twice, but: employers are busy as it is. They would really, really, REALLY prefer not to have to take an extra step of contacting you an extra time to get information you should've included from the beginning. (And hey, that's just if you answer the phone, which you probably won't, because who answers the fucking phone anymore when an unfamiliar number is calling? And how often do you check your email? Are you going to email me back RIGHT NOW, because RIGHT NOW is the time I've carved out in my constantly-busy-as-hell workweek to do this job of finding someone to give a job to, and you and your damned "Available Upon Request" is really holding me up and screwing up my schedule.)

If you think that mini-rant is over-the-top, I assure you it's not. That's the real-life scenario and thought process that will be happening around the person picking the next employee.

Just think about it: Is it really smart to try and force the employer to track you down and ask you for more information?

If you actually think that's OK, remember this: there are other strong resumes on my desk — resumes from people who actually chose to *include* references. I could choose another strong candidate, call his references right now, hire him, and still get out of my office before afternoon traffic hits and be saddled up to the bar at McPickleshitter's Irish Pub when happy hour starts.

Or I could try to call you and get some of these "upon request" references. Maybe I'll reach you — but maybe I'll get your voice mail. Or your girlfriend, your boyfriend, your mom, your dad, or your roommate. Maybe I'll leave a message (or maybe I'll just say forget it and hire the other guy). If I do leave a message, maybe you'll call back before I leave the office, but maybe not. And then when I come to work tomorrow, I've got another thing on my to-do list that I should've cleared off yesterday — and it's all because of your damned "references upon request" entry on your resume.

So again: What would you do if you were me? You'll hire the other guy, because he's thorough and he had a lot more respect for my time than you did!

A NOTE ABOUT REFERENCES AND THE ONE-PAGE RULE

As you've gathered from the last several pages of maniacal ranting, I'm adamant that you include your references and all their contact information on your resume. But if you've got three references complete with contact information, that can take up a lot of room, especially if you're stacking them vertically on top of one another.

It is not a mortal sin to add your references on a separate page. It's not my first choice — that would be for you to space them horizontally across the page on the same line. The only potential problem with putting references on a separate page is that it might get detached from your resume somehow and lost, but that's a risk you can be willing to take.

ANOTHER NOTE ABOUT REFERENCES AND PEOPLE ON THE INTERNET GIVING TERRIBLE ADVICE.

For better or worse, the Internet is open to everyone, including stupid people who are more than willing to give you very bad advice. For every piece of good advice I dole out in this book, I promise you can easily find someone on the Internet who will advise exactly the opposite. This is the nature of the Internet, and there's no changing it.

Unfortunately, some of these stupid people (or, to be fair, otherwise intelligent people whose advice is generally good but is unfortunately seasoned with pockets of stupidity) carry credentials that make them appear credible. Some have Ph.Ds, some write for employment websites, and still others are authors of books that are similar to this one. There are articles right now on Career Builder and other employment blogs that specifically state, *"Don't include references until and unless an employer asks you for them."*

This is literally, off-the-charts, insane advice. Bad advice from normal people with no connection to jobs and hiring is one thing; bad advice from people who are supposed to be expert sources of information is an entirely different level of shitty, and it really riles me up. These people who write this should be ashamed of themselves, because it's awful, negligent advice that's hurtful to the people they purport to help. I'd publicly shame them here, but most articles don't carry the name of the actual writer, which is a giant red flag. And of those who do actually put their names on the articles, most are bloggers or "consultants" who write about things they've never actually done in real life. Like hiring people.

In these cases, you're just going to have to decide who you trust the most. TRUST ME. I've hired more people and seen more resumes than all of them combined. But mostly, trust me because I'm right, and they're wrong.

TO PAD,
OR NOT TO PAD?
(OR, "YES, I INVENTED POST-IT NOTES.")

With all that talk about the thousands of new competitors you're going to have for every job thanks to the Internet, you're probably already thinking about padding your resume.

After all, I've been railing and railing on you about putting your best foot forward in this one concise page, right? So when the competition is this thick, should you push the envelope to add "extras" that might make the difference between a nice paycheck and another month living with your mom and dad?

Yes, you should.

It's my opinion that you should give yourself every reasonable advantage you can get away with. But padding your resume is an art. It's not something you can just do haphazardly and expect to get away with. There are some guidelines to follow when you're padding, and these guidelines will usually ensure that you give your resume some added "oomph" without opening yourself up to looking foolish or, at worst, getting fired later on.

And just so you hear it from me first — there's plenty of conflicting advice on this topic. Google "how to pad your resume" and you'll find more articles advising against it than advocating it. There are two reasons for this:

a) There will never be a shortage of self-righteous windbags ready to wag their finger at you for anything they perceive as a moral shortcoming. I have experienced this with my first book, Confessions of a Scholarship Judge, and I expect to receive it with this one as well. It's a good time to repeat the sole purpose of writing this book, and that is TO HELP YOU GET A JOB. It's not to get you to pass a polygraph test or to get you into heaven.

b) There's a lot of misinformation out there about what "padding" really is; or, at the very least, people have different definitions of the word. Like most people, I don't advocate out-and-out lying. But that's not what padding is.

WHAT PADDING IS, AND WHAT PADDING ISN'T

Padding means different things to different people. But hey, this is my book, so we're going to use my definition. Some people think "padding" means inventing jobs, skills and accomplishments out of thin air — jobs you never had, skills you don't begin to have and accomplishments you never accomplished — and adding them to beef up your resume.

That's not padding — that's just stupid. I'll explain why on the next few pages.

There's no perfect definition of smart resume padding, but here are a few principles which can be your guide.

PADDING PRINCIPLE 1: DON'T INCLUDE SKILLS YOU DON'T HAVE.

It bears repeating: a surprising many people think that padding your resume means making shit up out of thin air. They think that if they just pack enough BS into their resume, then they'll look like a major big shot to whom companies will want to make a big job offer right away.

But that's not quite how it works.

Companies are impressed not simply by skills, but by relevant skills: that is, skills that will help you perform well in the position you're applying for and help make the company more money. So if you're applying for a job as a floor supervisor at a manufacturing plant, it doesn't make sense to falsely claim that you speak French. I think most of us understand this.

But it makes even less sense to claim phony skills when they *are* relevant to the job. Let's say you're applying not for the manufacturing job; instead, you're applying for an international sales job. Lots of travel involved in Europe, where French is widely spoken (and not just in France). In this case, would claiming to speak French help you get the job? Absolutely. Should you do it?

Only if you're an idiot.

Why? Well, since French fluency is considered an asset, your bosses will expect you to do a good bit of French-speaking on the job then, won't they? And if you don't speak French, then you'll be found out rather quickly, wouldn't you say? You may not even make it past the interviewer if she decides to pop-quiz you with a little impromptu French conversation.

A disclosure is in order here. I made this boneheaded mistake myself several years ago. In the aftermath of the 9/11 attacks on the World Trade Center, business at my newly formed advertising agency was so slow that I was ready to give up and go back to getting a "real job" working for someone else. I sent out what seemed like 6,000 resumes, and one of the few responses I got was from Ryobi Outdoor Products.

Ryobi makes, among other things, lawn-care machinery like mowers, weed-whackers, chainsaws, etc., and there's a publications department within the company that handles all of the product manuals, from design to illustration to technical writing. They needed to hire a graphic designer for these manuals and wanted to bring me in for an interview.

I said OK. I wasn't much of a graphic designer anymore. It had been at least four years since I'd been employed as one. But I was quite literally going broke at this point — my only sources of income were donating plasma twice a week for $30 a pop and delivering Auto Traders to convenience stores in really bad neighborhoods every Wednesday night — so I was open to absolutely anything.

I interviewed well, and then went on a tour of the offices. They used Macintosh computers for all of their work, and although I hadn't used a Mac in years, that didn't worry me. I used Macs for years in the past, and they aren't hard to re-acquaint yourself with.

Then they handed me a manual for a lawnmower and told me I'd be responsible for producing similar documents. No biggie — I'd designed a couple hundred newsletters and literally thousands of newspaper pages in my life. Same shit, different topic.

I noticed the manuals all had very detailed drawings of the fully assembled machines, and dozens more drawings of every component of the machine. Every screw, bolt, handle, engine part, wheel, etc. I asked one of the designers where all these graphics came from — did they just have a giant library or database of component images? Man, this was going to be easy money.

Then she dropped the bomb on me. "We create them all in Illustrator."

As in, Adobe Illustrator, the program. I vaguely remembered having a couple of lessons in Illustrator when I was grad school, but they mostly consisted of drawing little more than glorified stick figures and getting the most rudimentary understanding of a program that is extremely powerful and complex.

Then I had my "OH SHIT" moment. It dawned on me that, in my post-9/11 desperation to pay my mortgage and my light bill and my car payment, I'd padded the living hell out of my resume. And one of the primary elements of my ill-advised resume padding was an entry in the "Skills" section, wherein I claimed that I was an expert with Adobe Illustrator.

Not proficient. Not competent. Not, "I can open the program and produce drawings that look like something a four-year-old drew with a crayon and stuck on the fridge." No — I said I was an *expert*.

In two seconds, I realized that I was utterly fucked. I needed the job and the money so, so badly — worse than I've ever needed money in my life. But there was no way I could do the job. My illustration skills were zero. They could've asked me to jump off the roof and soar around the parking lot like a pterodactyl, and I'd have had a better chance of pulling that off than illustrating lawnmower parts.

I bluffed my way through the rest of the interview and tour, told 'em it was no problem, and went about my merry way. Two days later they called and offered me the job. Yes, I actually GOT the job, which proves that the gift of being able to bullshit people can open more doors than you can possibly imagine.

But I couldn't take it. I would've walked in the door as a complete fraud from the word go, and I couldn't have lasted a week. Not even imminent poverty could make me go through with that. I never returned their calls. I just slouched off into the ether, never to be heard from again.

It happens every day — people padding their resumes with skills and claims so outlandish that they're caught almost immediately. Mine was accidental — I took the interview thinking it was a job I could actually do — but trust me, that didn't make me feel any less dumb.

Remember this: your immediate focus may be getting a job, but what you really want to do is *keep* a job. Don't make ridiculous claims on your resume just to help you get a job that you have no chance of keeping.

PADDING PRINCIPLE 2: IF YOU'VE HELD MULTIPLE POSITIONS AT THE SAME COMPANY, USE THE BEST ONE.

You may have started out in the mail room in 2003 and moved up to receptionist in 2004 and up to personnel manager in 2005, but you don't need to give details about every single step you've made in order to get where you currently are.

Far more important than the mundane details of your ascent are the details and responsibilities of your current position. So, rather than a resume entry that looks like this:

Acme Corporation
Personnel Manager, February 2005 — present
Receptionist, April 2004 — January 2005
Mail Room, November 2003 — March 2004

Try this:

Personnel Manager
Acme Corporation
November 2003 - present

This is smart padding.

Did you lie? No. Did you work as the personnel manager at Acme Corporation? Yes, and you still do. Did you work at Acme from November 2003 — present? Absolutely. Did you arrange the information in such a way that the employer — you hoped, anyway — would believe you'd been the personnel manager since November 2003? Yes — and that's smart padding for you.

Will the employer call you on it — will he ask you if you were indeed the personnel manager the whole time? It's unlikely — he has no reason to believe otherwise. But even if he does, it's not a big deal. You simply answer: "Actually, Acme moved me around to assist in a couple of other departments during my first few months before they settled me into my personnel manager position." And that's the absolute truth.

And what if he presses you? Again, it's unlikely, but let's be prepared. Which other departments, he asks? And you rattle off several: "Accounting (or wherever you were a receptionist), HR, Marketing, Communications (that's the mail room). I asked to see the workings of as many departments as I could, so I could get a comprehensive feel for what the company does."

That's a glorious piece of bullshitting right there — truly excellent stuff. Not only did you hide the fact you only recently became a personnel manager, but you also made yourself look great with that whole "show me how this company works" bit.

That's a great angle, by the way. Whether it's a job with a huge company or a tiny mom-and-pop shop or a recreational soccer team — the more you understand about how all the other people do their jobs, the better you'll understand how to do yours. Most people don't realize this, and many try to stay as far away from the other parts of the company as possible, so it's impressive when someone like you comes along who really wants to understand how things work.

The point here is this: although your experience may seem unimpressive to you, it can still seem very impressive to prospective employers if you just know how to frame the information correctly. A Burger King shift manager may believe she has a very mundane existence and nothing that would impress an employer. But in the world of resume-speak, she's got all this going for her:

- Oversees weekly grossly sales of $30-$35k
- Responsible for staff of 25
- Face-to-face interaction with 1,500+ customers weekly
- Generates daily sales and labor reports

Sounds a lot more exciting on paper than in the real world, eh? But that's the point — resumes are supposed to make you sound powerful, accomplished and ready to take the next job by the horns.

And contrary to what many applicants think, employers don't have a sixth sense for detecting resume padding — they WANT to believe what you say. It's extremely rare to sit down for an interview with someone who's trying to excavate fibs from your resume. Much more often than not, they're very eager to talk to you and are crossing their fingers that you'll be great and they'll get the chance to hire you.

Here's a real-life example of this padding principle from my own resume.

When I got out of graduate school in 1999, I went to work for Cox Interactive Media, a company that had online city guides in a couple dozen cities. I was hired by the Phoenix site, AccessArizona.com, as a "content producer" — essentially, a late-'90s cross between a webmaster and a marketer and a journalist. My starting salary was $35,000, which equates to exactly $50,000 in 2014 dollars.

They hired me to manage the Travel and Recreation sections of our site, which entailed posting one story with accompanying photos once a week. I'm serious, once a week. That's it. That was my job.

Oh yeah, and I didn't write the stories or take the pictures. We paid freelancers to do that. I was just the guy that put it up on the website.

I worked 11 a.m. to 8 p.m., Wednesday through Sunday. Sometimes I'd go play nine holes of golf before I even came to work. On my lunch break, I'd work out in the gym that was in the bottom of our building. Hop in the elevator, hit "basement" and bang, I'm in the gym. It's the only gym I ever belonged to that actually provided *clothes* for you to work out in. It was like a P.E. uniform from the 1960s, but still, how awesome is that?

On Saturdays and Sundays, I was the only person in the office all day long — I unlocked the shop in the morning and locked it up on my way out. I listened to music all day, surfed the web at high-speed (that was a rare luxury in 1999) and drank all the free Starbucks I wanted. On the weekends, I admit that an occasional nap was taken. Ball games of all types were watched at my preferred television volume.

Long story short, it was fucking awesome. Never has being the low man on the totem pole been so satisfying.

Cushy working conditions notwithstanding, I do remember putting my nose to the grindstone a little. After all, it was my first job out of graduate school, and I was determined to let all these Arizona State graduates around me know what a superior crop of people the Missouri School of

Journalism was producing.

I took on extra work. After all, I had plenty of time to help out; it took me all of 45 minutes to post that one Travel story per week. If things were going rough for the other section producers in the evenings, I'd hang out until 9, 10, or even later if they needed help. Again, it's not like I needed to be up early in the morning. Christ, I didn't come in until lunchtime. I'd just moved to Phoenix and had absolutely no social life, so I was happy to score points with the bigwigs for giving freely of my time.

About three months later, my immediate supervisor — an incredible lady named Claudine Langan who went on to a great career in media and now real estate — got a promotion. She was getting sent to Las Vegas to open up a new site in a new town, and she got to name her successor.

She chose me, and bumped my pay to $40k ($57k by today's standards). Total shock, but of course I was overjoyed. Who goes from worst to first after three months on the job?

But as you might imagine, the six other producers I leap-frogged were less than overjoyed. I was an amiable guy and I think they liked me as a person, but it wasn't enough to keep them around after being passed over for the guy who just got out of college. One by one, most left the company over the next few months. I didn't blame them; they were all very smart and talented people and opportunities were everywhere back then.

But those of us who hung around didn't despair; we just tried to become more efficient with the people we had. Eventually, about a year after my original hire date, I was promoted again, this time to "Content Manager." My duties didn't change, but my salary got bumped to $60,000 ($85k in 2014 money). Also, in terms of the company as a whole, I outranked my peers who held similar positions in cities like Seattle, Miami, Atlanta, etc.

Life was good, but there was trouble on the horizon. Our entire staff was in the meeting room one day for a conference call with our CEO, who announced next year's objective: take 50% of Yahoo's local market share.

Yes, you read that correctly: take not 5%, but 50% market share — from the most popular website on the planet at that time. In one year.

Apparently venture capitalists weren't the only ones smoking crack during the first Internet boom.

Gee whiz, why don't we wipe out world hunger while we're at it?

I wasn't the only one in our office who thought the idea was nuts, but apparently I was the only one who thought it was so *incredibly* nuts that it was time to get the hell out of there right away, while my position at AccessArizona.com still carried some cachet and before Yahoo! and AOL bitch-slapped us into obscurity quicker than you can say "Pets-dot-com." I snapped up a job at a software company across town for $75,000 ($105k in today's dollars) and abruptly bid AccessArizona.com adieu.

I went into great detail there so that you could see the difference between what actually happened at my Access Arizona job vs. how it ended up looking on my resume. In reality, it went like this:

I got hired as low man on the totem pole, enjoyed leisurely weekends on the clock, got a quick promotion based on my boss getting her own promotion and that boss making the highly irregular move of jumping me up into her job. I trudged through a few months, got another promotion, then bolted like an escaped fugitive at the first sign of trouble.

But you can bet my resume tells a different story. Here's my entry for that period:

Content & Marketing Manager, AccessArizona.com
AccessArizona.com
May 1999-October 2000

- Responsible for all content and marketing operations for Phoenix city site and 12 partner sites, drawing 150,000+ unique users and 3.5 million page views/month
- Managed content, graphics, marketing and technical staff of 12
- Supervised the implementation of all corporate e-commerce and advertising initiatives
- Supervised design and creation of partner sites and advertiser microsites, including Power 92, The Zone, The Edge, KGME, Xtra Sports 910, KFYI, Bucky's Casino, Prescott Resort, Cox 9, Greater Phoenix Ford Stores, Honda of Tempe, etc.
- Managed content for multiple advertiser accounts

- Wrote weekly email newsletter
- Responsible for monthly & yearly usage targets

It's all true, and it sounds a hell of a lot better than the previous paragraph, doesn't it? I worked hard and everything, don't get me wrong, but that resume makes me look WAY busier and more managerial and more serious than I was. I mean, look at that entry. Does that look like a guy who literally *slept* on the job occasionally?

Notice that I have one position listed, and that's the last and best-paying one. I even beefed it up with the part about being the marketing manager, which I'll talk more about in a second. But in dozens of job interviews I've had with this resume, not once has anyone asked even one question about whether I was "Content & Marketing Manager" during my entire period of employment at Cox Interactive.

By the way: a year later, Cox Interactive Media was out of business, eaten alive by competition. Which leads me to my next principle:

PADDING PRINCIPLE 3: IF THE COMPANY ON YOUR RESUME NO LONGER EXISTS, THEN YOU'VE GOT MORE LEEWAY WHEN PADDING.

This is especially useful for those of you who were working, or at least in college, during the heyday of the Internet. If you worked in an industry that was even close to being associated with the Internet, chances are you did some work for a company that doesn't exist today.

That was a real downer back then, but it does have some usefulness today. Ever heard the phrase "dead men tell no tales"? It applies here.

If I were applying for a job today, I'd certainly list my experience and achievements at Cox Interactive. But there's no place for a potential employer to call and verify anything I say on my resume. The phones are disconnected. The offices are now occupied by completely different companies. Every employee is with some other company, and many of them have left the industry altogether. There's no one to call.

This is inconvenient for your prospective employer, but it can be very helpful for the enterprising resume padder. It enables you to do things like beef up the name of your position a little, like I did above with "Content & Marketing Manager." We had a marketing manager and it wasn't me, but that doesn't matter anymore. There's no one around to dispute it, and even if you managed to track down my old bosses, they probably wouldn't remember the details well enough to contradict me anyway.

A defunct previous company also allows you, on paper, to assume the job duties of somebody else that you worked with. For example, let's say your cubicle neighbor at your old job was Robert McPickleshitter (no relation to Jane). You sat next to Robert and talked to him every day for two years, so you know exactly what his job responsibilities were.

Now, fast-forward to the present day. Would Robert's job responsibilities look good on your resume? Furthermore — and I can't stress this part enough — are you familiar with the ins and outs of those responsibilities, and can you actually perform those responsibilities? If the answer is yes, then I recommend adding them to your resume as padding.

Make no mistake here: this is lying. If you're morally opposed to lying in all situations, then you're going to want to skip this one. However, if you're like most people a hind willing to bend the truth a little in a situation where there's no realistic chance of getting caught, then follow along.

If you can do the job just as well as Robert did it, and neither Robert nor your boss is around any longer to prove otherwise, then for all practical purposes, you might as well say you did it. Your prospective employer would strongly disagree if he/she could read this over your shoulder, but who cares? This is a section on padding. What he doesn't know won't hurt him.

And let's be practical here: if you can truly do the job, why would anyone's suspicion ever be aroused? If you claim Robert's job of doing weekly budget reports in Quickbooks, and during your first week on the job you crank out some masterful Quickbooks projects for your new boss — what is there to be suspicious of? Will your boss come over to your desk and say, "Wow, Jane, these are excellent Quickbooks reports, and you really are excellent at Quickbooks, just like you said on your resume. BUT….did you REALLY do those Quickbooks reports at your last job, or were you padding your resume?" Of course not.

Remember, I'm talking about job *responsibilities* here, not job title. It's a lot easier to fly under the radar by simply adding these responsibilities under the heading for a position you actually did hold — or, as in my case above, for a position whose title has been modified only slightly. On the rare chance that you meet up with someone who worked with you and Robert McPickleshitter and happened to be examining your resume, she might remember your job title and Robert's job title and smell a rat. On the other hand, would she remember every little detail of every task that you and Robert performed? Not likely.

PADDING PRINCIPLE 4: USE POWERFUL CREATIVE WORDING TO CREATE STRONG ENTRIES.

This isn't only a principle of padding; it's a principle of good resume writing and, for that matter, all good writing. But I mean to take it a step further here in our padding section to remind you that even seemingly frivolous or even fun things you've done on the job can be described as a highfalutin' responsibility that you never failed to meet. Let me give you another real-life example.

During my time at the aforementioned Cox Interactive, I attended a weeklong senior producers' conference at our home base in Atlanta. We had plenty of time to interact with senior company management and we had some seminars to attend, but the overarching theme of the conference was to get together with other senior producers to share ideas: ideas about how to make our sites more successful and how to manage and motivate our people (which I really needed, since many of my people were still bristling about my promotion).

That's the idea, anyway. But the company failed to realize what happens when two dozen 20-somethings with company Amex cards get plucked from their jobs and whisked off to a 4-star hotel in an exciting city for a week. More than a little cutting loose took place.

We got together, all right, and to be fair, we did shoot the breeze about our jobs quite a bit. But most of it came after our heads were clouded with multiple mixed drinks, and even then, we were usually just bitching about our bosses, bitching about our employees or bitching about how far our corporate management had its head up its ass (we were right on the latter). And I recall a handful of my colleagues stumbling off to spend the night in rooms that were not their own. Oh, the scandal!

Thanks to this drunken carrying on, very little was learned in our early-morning seminars, other than where the closest drugstore was located that sold Halls cough drops to get that awful gin smell off our breath (answer: hotel lobby store). Late morning seminars weren't much better. Afternoon seminars were skipped in favor of a little nap therapy.

In retrospect, I'm surprised we learned anything at all during the entire week. But this kind of stuff happens at conferences all the time. If the conference involves young people, multiply it by 3. If it involves the marketing profession, multiply it by 8.

Now, what does this have to do with your resume? Well, just because my conference turned out to be little more than 25 booze-soaked Internet yuppies groping each other for a week doesn't mean that it can't make a meaningful statement on my resume.

Here's what the bullet point looks like for this week of hellraising:

- Led a team of nationwide studio managers tasked with advising corporate management about identifying and solving field-level challenges.

YYYYEEEAAAHHH! Try that on for size! That's what a week of company-paid eating, drinking and being merry looks like on my resume. If you're not applauding right now, you should be.

You may not have an analogous example here for your own resume, but don't miss my overall point here, which is: If you're like most people, you're prone to overlook opportunities to make yourself look good on your resume.

What I remember most of the above week was the fun stuff, and I didn't "lead" that group of managers any more than anyone else did. But that's irrelevant. I was, in fact, brought to Atlanta to talk with my peers nationwide and to share our concerns with our corporate overlords — and that's what my resume says I did. No need to dwell on the boozing and shenanigans.

If you think hard, you've probably got your own version of the above alchemy that can turn a fun retreat or conference or vacation or whatever into some primo resume padding. Think hard, and if it suits your purposes, include it.

TIDY UP YOUR WEB RESUME.

(OR, "YES, THOSE ARE STILL A THING, LINKEDIN NOTWITHSTANDING)

Long, long ago, in a place called 1997, both the education and business worlds alike were buzzing about Web resumes. Just to clarify, I'm not referring to the ability to email someone your current resume, or to upload it to an online storehouse of resumes like Monster or Career Builder. When I say "Web resume," I'm talking about creating a Web page that is the "interactive" version of your resume, replete with links, work samples, and other technical wizardry now accessible and easily mastered by even the most delicate technophobes.

Web resumes were going to change the world of employment forever. Paper resumes would disappear forever, and consequently, forests full of trees would be saved. More importantly, desks would no longer be littered with thousands of resumes and hundreds of folders and sticky notes to manage them. Millions of dollars in postage would be saved on the U.S. Postal Service, who would no longer be relied upon for overpriced, slow-motion delivery of the critical documents that shaped our very financial futures.

Now, employers would have to go no further than the nearest computer to call up your resume, review in full-color detail your most impressive accomplishments and click an email link to offer you a job. OfficeMax would file for bankruptcy. Mail carriers would all have to become pizza delivery drivers. Panic would ensue. Chaos would reign.

Unfortunately, none of that happened. Which is a huge bummer, really, because that all sounded like a pretty interesting change of pace. Not only that, but I had a personal stake in it as well. Back in 1998, the University of Missouri paid my way through graduate school (under the highbrow-sounding "Pulitzer New Media Fellowship," no less) to teach students how to create wonderful, effective Web resumes. I was a pioneer in this burgeoning art, and besides that, do you know how expensive grad school is?

But Web resumes never really caught fire, and now I'm hawking this book on Amazon for $10. Sorry about that, Pulitzer family.

What happened to Web resumes? They're still around, and I still recommend you create one (otherwise you wouldn't be reading this). But as it turns out, just like in many other areas of life that have become more "computerized," the result was a drastic increase in printing and paper usage, rather than a decrease. It seems that folks just like to print stuff out, presumably to take it with them on the subway, on vacation, to the toilet, or whatever.

Looking back, that seems really obvious (Warning: If you didn't get filthy rich on Internet stocks, do not look directly back at 1998 for long periods of time. It can cause ulcers).

Yes indeed, people like to print. But most people tossing those Web resumes together didn't make them very printer-friendly. They got crazy with big graphics and fonts and colors and shading and bolding and even (gasp!) animation. So when Big Boss Lady printed this beautiful screen gem on their standard-issue, black-and-white ink-jet printer, it looked like an absolute mess and ended up in the trash can.

But it's not just printer-unfriendliness that kept Web resumes from getting big (that can be fixed, and I'll show you how). Drunk on the possibilities that new technology brings, people got a little too crazy with their newfound power and monkeyed around with their resumes a little too much.

Remember our guiding principle of only including relevant information in your resume? Well, a Web resume, with its ability to link to any site in the world, just begs you to include extra junk.

HERE ARE 3 QUICK WAYS TO SCREW UP A WEB RESUME:

1) **Link to everything you possibly can, regardless of importance.** Why list Palookaville State University in your "Education" section without hyperlinking it to the PSU home vpage? Sure, it has absolutely no relevance or useful information for your employer, but why let that stop you?

   Same goes for any club memberships you've listed, teams you've been a member of. Do they have websites? Then why not link to them?

   Because it's a distraction and the information behind those links is useless. The home page of your university is no more relevant than linking to the home page of Wal-Mart or Applebee's or the Facebook page of your favorite bar.

2) **Three words: Logos, logos, logos.** Your school has a logo. So do all of the companies you've worked for in the past. Why not include them in your Web resume? A computer user's eye is involuntarily drawn to images, so your potential employer will be forced to pay attention to them whether he/she wants to or not.

   And while you're at it, don't forget to link those logos to their corresponding websites (see item 1). That way, you can have two links to each site instead of just one!

   Logos on Web resumes are dumb. Unless you're a graphic designer and you actually designed those logos yourself, leave them off. They add nothing to the discussion except clutter.

3) **Be sure to leave "crumbs" to your private, often embarrassing, personal information.** If your Web resume resides on a page of your personal website, be sure to make it easy to find the rest of your site in just a click or two: you and three half-naked friends hitting a bong, your blog about which professors you hate, your audio and video files that may or may not be legally obtained, etc.

   Preserve the image of yourself as a professional AT LEAST until you get the job. If absolutely necessary, you can tear it down later.

Having said all that, it may surprise you to know that my overall advice about linking to personal information is actually pretty contrarian and not nearly as uptight as the previous pages would suggest. Let me clarify for you while you consider the following information that you should link to on your Web resume:

1) **Link to your Facebook page.** That's right, do link to your Facebook page. You know why? Because every diligent employer is going to sniff it out anyway. The explosion of social media over the last 10 years is a treasure trove for employers, and we know how to gather loads of information on you in ways we never could have before.

   So be up-front and make it easy by just including your Facebook profile to begin with. That does NOT mean you have to open up your privacy settings so that the world can see everything about you. No one expects that of you, and even if they did, you don't owe it to loosen your personal privacy preferences so that some nosy Big Boss Lady can check out the details of your life that she doesn't have any right to.

   HOWEVER...if you do have loose privacy settings, then you can bet your right arm that employers will be enthusiastically perusing your photos and posts. Why? Because they definitely give you an insight into the real person behind the resume — the real person you'll have to deal with day in and day out, and that information is GOLD to an employer. Even better than the resume sometimes.

   Given that, here's a short list of stuff I consider useful information when sniffing out a job applicant on Facebook. Use this list as a guide for what you may want to include and what you may want to hide.

- Drinking doesn't bother me in the least. Finger-waggers everywhere advise you to hide all photos of yourself drinking when you're trying to get a job, but I disagree. If you're 21 and there are pictures of you drinking beer at a game or wine at a restaurant and you're generally not acting like a complete drunken mess, that's not something to worry about. If you're doing a keg stand in swimwear while being groped by two friends, that's another story. I'd hide those. Got a pic of you leaning your face down over six tequila shots before you pound them all in succession? Might want to hide that one, too. If you're drinking underage, I'd hide those, too. But social, responsible alcohol use is a practice you'll share with a majority of your colleagues, so don't worry too much about those.

- If you're using drugs in any photos — or even if you're not, but you're around others who are — hide those. And even though weed is well on the way to being legal everywhere (and as I write this is legal in Washington and Colorado), it's too soon to assume employers everywhere are going to be cool with it. Some of the most talented and valuable people I've ever worked with are regular pot smokers and I personally couldn't care less if someone who worked for me smoked when they weren't on the clock, but trust me, this is still a minority opinion. Don't tempt fate here.

- Social media behavior that's far more dangerous to your employment prospects are the things that tag you is that which tags you as just a generally unpleasant human being. Do your profiles indicate that you're whiny, negative, a drama queen, an attention whore or just kind of an asshole? If so, this is WAY more harmful than any picture of you drinking beer.

If every third Facebook post is you bitching about someone or something or how men suck or women suck or the world is going to hell...forget it. Office cancer in the making.

Same with people who air every bit of their personal drama. Example: *"Some people need to know when to shut their mouth and mind their own business and move on with their lives! You know who you are!"* Yep, you're right, and I'll be moving on from your application and minding my own business and never considering you again for one second.

Same with people who take 800 selfies and make a new one their profile picture every day groveling for compliments. Example: *"New hair and new cute dress I just got, what do you guys think?"* I think you're one of those people who needs constant coddling and ego boosts just to make it through a regular day.

Same with people who bash their current employer. *"OMG my boss is such a dick...so SICK of working night shift! My job sucks!"* Great. So excited to be your next boss!

You didn't think about all this being a factor in getting a job, did you? Well, you're welcome, because they are. Employers are real people who will be spending more hours with you per week than your own family and friends, and no one wants to spend that much time around people who are INSUFFERABLY IRRITATING.

- Watch your politics, too. If you're an outspoken Tea Party supporter applying for a job in a room full of left-leaning cyclists who would slit their wrists before putting a plastic water bottle in the regular trash can instead of the recycling bin — you are not gonna get that job if the incumbents read all about that on Facebook. On the flip side, if you openly embrace Obamacare and have signed 8 petitions against Monsanto's genetically altered food and your potential bosses still want to see Obama's birth certificate, you're not going to get that job either. And you'll never know why you didn't get the job, but that'll be why (or at least it'll be a convenient way to eliminate you as a candidate).

  No one else will admit this to you openly, but trust me, it happens every day. If your Facebook or any other social profiles are open, beware of all the above.

2) **Link to your LinkedIn profile.** This assumes you have an LinkedIn profile, and if you don't, go make one right away. Remember how I said that all your potential employers will be sniffing through your Facebook profile? Well, they won't be

doing that until after they've looked at your LinkedIn profile, because LinkedIn is the universe's one-stop shop for professional networking. If you don't have a LinkedIn profile, you're not serious about getting a job.

A LinkedIn profile doesn't replace a resume. Despite having pretty much all the same information on it, employers are still asking for resumes, so that's that. But it's the place where potential employers evaluate you before they get your resume (if they know you'll be sending one), and they definitely look at your LinkedIn profile after they get your resume, just to further vet you. (And not for nothing, almost everyone has a picture on their LinkedIn profile, which pretty much destroys any argument against attaching one to your resume).

3) **Link to your work samples.** This is the primary value of a Web resume.

Whether your resume is exemplary or mediocre or a total piece of garbage, resumes are still all talk and no action. You can talk a big game all over a resume, but there's still no space for actual work you've done.

That's where Web resumes come in. You can show your future bosses the real stuff you've actually done.

This is easy if you're a writer or a designer or a photographer or any other job that yields digital files you can link to your resume. But it works for just about everyone else, too, if you think about it creatively.

If you're a programmer, you can link to the programs you've created. If you're any kind of planner or strategist in any industry, you can link to documents you've created.

But it doesn't just work for white-collar folks. My cousin Tim Malson is a master bricklayer and stonemason in Nashville (if you need one of those and you're down in those parts, look up Malson Masonry). You know what's on his resume and other marketing materials? Work samples!

In photo form, of course. There are before and after pictures of everything a bricklayin' guy can do, from fireplaces to landscaping work to entire houses he rebuilt after Hurricane

Katrina. Those are work samples.

You can be a Craig's List handyman or housecleaner, and you can and should post work samples. Work samples are simply before and after pictures: a leaky roof vs. a fixed roof, a decrepit old deck with peeling paint vs. a freshly sanded and stained deck, a disgustingly cluttered house worthy of a "Hoarders" episode vs. a sparkling, exquisitely organized place.

Everyone can do work samples. Well, except maybe embalmers. Probably wouldn't be good to post photos of your freshly spruced-up dead folks on the Internet (although you could still send them privately).

So there you have it. Unless you work in a funeral home, post work samples on your Web resume and show your future employers the hard evidence that you can do — and, indeed, have done — whatever they require.

THE OBLIGATORY COVER LETTER SECTION

(OR, "NECESSARY EVILS ARE STILL NECESSARY. AND EVIL.")

It seems like every job opening out there requires you to send a cover letter with your resume, doesn't it?

This is not because cover letters are terribly insightful; they aren't. In fact, it's very rare that anyone ever reads them very carefully, and often they're simply detached from the resume and tossed into the trash without a second glance. Despite this, most HR departments continue to require them just because they always have, and why change now, right?

But cover letters are still a fact of life, so we have to address them. After all, you don't want to be caught with your pants down when that one boss out there who actually cares about these things is the person you're trying to impress. Here are some guidelines for cover letters that people actually read:

1) **Make it snappy.** Five paragraphs? Hell no. It's a cover letter, not a cover novella. This is just a segue to your resume, so you don't want to rehash the entire thing in paragraph form. Instead, be sharp, snappy, brief and to the point.

2) **Address the needs of the employer.** Most cover letters talk about me, me, me. "I'm a student at" so-and-so, and "I enjoy this" and "I'd like to join the team," etc.

All of that may be true, but respectfully, what you like is not super-important to me. Those statements don't speak directly to my needs as an employer, and you're only here submitting a resume because *I need something.*

All employers want you to help them create more of two things: money and time. Don't say this: "I am Jane McPickleshitter and I'm a Widget-making major at Arizona State University, where I enjoy making widgets and look forward to enhancing my widget-making skills and learning even more about widgets."

First of all, never tell an employer you want the job so you can *learn.* I've read countless cover letters and resumes by well-intentioned applicants who blather on about how this job is in the widget-making industry and they've always loved widgets and they want to learn all about widgetry and they can't wait to come to my widget-making job and just learn, learn, learn. Hooray for learning!

No. Learning is what happens elsewhere, before you get here. It's what qualifies you to apply for the job in the first place. Sure, you'll have to be trained and "learn" the way we do things around here, but other than that, the less *learning* you have to do on my dime, the more attractive job candidate you are.

Second of all, I know what your name is and I know where you go to school. It's already on your resume. This isn't the place to rehash elementary facts. This is where you hook me with some compelling statement that makes me want to read more.

Instead, say: "I can immediately take over the widget-making responsibilities at Widgets, Inc., and I'll develop new widget-making efficiencies that can lead to cost savings for the company." That's a bold statement, but I'll take a bold statement any day. If I want details on how you plan to do this, I'll ask you in the interview.

But you know what that means? It means you *got an interview.* The other 95% of applicants won't.

3) **I think? I can.** There's a very subtle element of language that makes a huge difference in not only the way you're perceived by others, but in what you yourself can achieve (not to get all Tony Robbins on you, but it's true).

Here it is: on one hand, there are statements like "I think I can," "I'll try to," "I'll do my best," "I'll attempt to," etc. On the other hand are two, and only two, far superior phrases: "I can" and "I will." The first phrases well-intentioned but also communicate doubt. And here's something that a lot of your future employers (myself included) believe: The people who doubt themselves in the beginning will often fail to deliver in the end.

That may sound harsh, but it's true — the more "wiggle room" you allow yourself from the beginning by hedging your statements with things like "I'll try" or "I'll do my best," the more likely you are to use that room to wiggle out of your commitment in the end when things get difficult.

I am not a Star Wars fan, but one of my favorite lines is from Yoda in *The Empire Strikes Back:* "Do or do not. There is no try." That's exactly right: you'll either do something or you won't, and that's that. And 99% of whether you do it or not is your own attitude about the task before you start.

It's outside the scope of this book to go into detail about how to get the right attitude, but this book is about resumes, so for our purposes, you only need to look like you have the right attitude on paper. And the way to do that is to catch yourself saying "I think I can" and "I'll try to" and change them to "I can" and "I will."

4) **Address the recipient by name.** Find out the name of the person in charge of hiring for the position, then address that person by name in your letter.

You'll have to do a little more work — you won't just get to print 100 copies of the same letter with a "To Whom It May Concern" heading. But you shouldn't be sending those if you have an alternative. "To Whom It May Concern" is what people write when they're too lazy to figure out who the letter should be addressed to.

Taking an extra 60 seconds to enter the addressee's full name informs the employer that you're not just dumping resumes all over the world and hoping something will stick. People who do so are not prime candidates for employment. They are the crack whores of the job market. *"What you want? What you need? You got money? You got a paycheck? If you got money, I'll do it, honey!"*

I speak from experience, because I've been there myself. Not crack whoring (although that wasn't far off on the horizon back in the Ryobi lawnmower days), but cropdusting the world with my resume when I was out of work and badly needed a gig. Notice that I've never said it's bad to do the resume cropdusting — it's only bad to appear that you're resume cropdusting. Sometimes you just need work, and you'll do whatever pays the bills.

But now think of the employer. If he knows that you're dropping your resume on any desk that isn't occupied by a schoolchild, what does that mean to him? Well, like I said above — it means you're not interested in HIS work, but rather any work that will restock your cabinets with mac-and-cheese. And of course, employers would much rather hire someone who's actually interested in their business than someone who's just passing by for a paycheck until something better comes along.

5. **Google the person you're writing to and dig up something interesting about him/her.** Use it in your letter.

Remember that part about potential employers sniffing you out on Facebook and LinkedIn? Yeah, well, two can play at that game. And you should play, too. Just like those sites are a goldmine for employers doing their due diligence on you, they might be even better tools for you.

It is amazing, however, how few job applicants actually do this. Most do absolutely no research whatsoever on the person they'll be interacting with. But their loss is your gain: investigating your employer can give you tons of insight on a lot of different things, but most importantly for our purposes here, how you can get that person to hire you.

Read their LinkedIn and Facebook profiles carefully, and Google them as well. Collect the basics: where they went to school, where they used to work, previous positions they've held at any company, etc. Where did he/she go to school? If they've ever written any articles or blog posts about the industry you're both in, read every one you can find.

This serves two purposes. First, it's a great way of getting to know someone and feeling familiar with them, even if you haven't met them (If this feels like stalking to you, chill; remember, they're already doing it to you, too). Second, it can give you valuable crumbs of information about his/her perspectives on both the large and small aspects of the job.

In your letter, work in your new knowledge. You don't have to be subtle about it — the boss won't think you're a stalker. This is the kind of thing you're *supposed* to do before you apply, because it shows you care enough about getting the job to spend extra time researching the position and the company.

Quick example: Let's say I was applying for a job as a media buyer (someone who decides where advertising money does and doesn't get spent) and I found a blog post my potential boss wrote about how he thinks local TV and radio advertising are usually a giant waste of money. That's an opinion I agree with, so I'd do my best to work that into my letter and build some common ground. The sooner this guy knows I share his opinion about wasting money in these areas, the better off I am from the get-go.

Let's also say I've discovered that he attended the University of Florida, he's a big fan of Gator football, and that he rose through the ranks pretty quickly at his current company.

You can be creative about how you work this information into your letter, or you can just be direct, which can work very nicely. Something like this:

Dear Mr. McPickleshitter:

Even the most talented teams can go only so far without a strong leader. Only those that combine top-flight talent and the leadership to develop that talent find high-level success. I've chosen to build my career with a company that's geared for that type of long-term success, and although we've yet to meet in person, I'm confident in saying I'm an asset that'll fit your team well and help you grow, and you're the right leader for me.

Your ascent from media buyer to Vice President of Strategic Media Planning at Acme Advertising in three years tells me that Acme believes you've got vision. I have vision, too: I share your outlook on the declining cost-effectiveness of radio and TV ads, and I think we'd work well together. A possible exception would be October 15th, when my Missouri Tigers play the Gators in football, but I promise not to gloat if we win, and to eat crow if we lose.

I hope my attached resume leaves you as optimistic as I am, and I hope to speak in person soon.

Best regards,
Josh Barsch

That's pretty good. I flipped it around a little bit. Mr. McPickleshitter opened up my letter thinking I'd be trying to sell myself to him, but I ended up selling him as a good boss/match for me. If you were Mr. McPickleshitter, you might like me already. But even if you weren't quite ready to like me yet, you're not gonna be forgetting me anytime soon. I talked about stuff that's completely different from what the other applicants talked about, and not for nothing, I made him laugh at least once. That's always good.

Here's an example of how NOT to work your research into your cover letter:

Dear Mr. McPickleshitter:

Even the most talented teams can go only so far without a strong leader. But you already know this; your wife April and your daughters Hannah Jane and Twyla Sue surely look up to you as the fearless leader of the McPickleshitter clan. Not to mention your post as Vice President of the Palookaville Heights Neighborhood Association, where I'm sure people drop by your place at 4316 Spring St. to bounce their concerns off you. I'm confident in saying I'm an asset that'll fit your team well and help you grow, and you're the right leader for me.

I hope my attached resume leaves you as optimistic as I am, and I hope to speak in person soon. Maybe at Copeland's, where you gave the fried calamari po-boy 5 stars on Yelp last Thursday? I'm game if you are.

Best regards,
Josh Barsch

Yep, that's well beyond creepy. Just because you know it, doesn't mean you mention it.

OVERALL, LET'S SUMMARIZE THE COVER LETTER HERE:

- **Be brief.**

- **Be personal.**

- **Be unique.**

- **Be punchy.**

- **Do your research.**

If you do all this, you'll have a huge leg up on most of your competitors.

MORE GREAT ADVICE
NO ONE'S GIVEN YOU
(OR, "STUFF NOT QUITE LONG
ENOUGH FOR A FULL CHAPTER")

Use a real email address with your real name in it. As in, *firstname.lastname@gmail.com*. That's very straightforward, safe, and easy to remember. You can't go wrong with this kind of email address.

Remember how we've talked about the need to stand out from the competition? Yeah, your email address is not the place to do it. Do not spend hours putting together a great resume and then ruin your professional image by putting down *phatbootyshaka@aol.com* (actually any AOL address will make you look like a dinosaur, so please don't do that) or *demonicoverlord420@yahoo.com*. Or *goyankees@yahoo.com* or liljenfurreal@msn.com or anything you thought was totally cute six years ago when you first got it.

Yes, but: "I don't have an email address that's just my first and last name like that!" Then create one, and use it for all job-related correspondence. I'm a Gmail fan myself, but Yahoo! and Live.com (or Outlook.com or whatever Microsoft is calling its latest crappy service these days) is fine too.

I once had a student send me a resume, cover letter and everything — with a from line/email address of "Piggy Forgetful." Seriously, and presumably with a straight face, writing me for a job and then signing her letter PIGGY FORGETFUL.

I have no idea what gets into some people.

(Piggy, if you're out there reading this and the name on your birth certificate is actually Piggy Forgetful...please forgive me. But I've Googled you in the years since receiving your email and I've found no trace of you, so I assume you've gone back to using your given name. Kudos.)

Use an attractive design for your resume. Don't just type-and-center like all the other boring people do.

Do you know how many things in life are done the way they're done simply because that's the way they've always been done and nobody's had good sense enough to rock the boat? LOTS, that's how many.

One of those things is using a shitty, boring, ugly resume that's text and nothing else.

Almost everyone does this, but you don't have to. There's no rule that says you can't jazz things up a little with a very nice, visually attractive design that makes your resume stand out from the pile.

Don't feel bad if you haven't thought of this; most people don't do it. I've reviewed resumes not only from students and entry-level people, but from top-flight CEOs applying for high 6-figure/low 7-figure executive positions — dudes who were WAY above my pay grade — that were absolutely HIDEOUS, boring documents that made the most accomplished businesspeople look like boring schmoes off the street.

Don't be one of those. Jazz it up a little.

And don't worry, you don't have to be a designer yourself to pull this off. There are professional designers all over the world who are waiting at this very moment to build you a really attractive resume for as little as $5. I'm serious. I highly recommend Fiverr.com, a worldwide marketplace of insanely skilled people who are willing to do amazing things for the low, low price of — you guessed it — $5.

As a guy who practices what he preaches, I have multiple resumes. I'm not seeking a professional job, but I'm interested in doing some college teaching on the side and I also do some expert witnessing in criminal cases. I used Fiverr to have people design resumes for me for both of those endeavors, and they are the loveliest resumes I've ever had. They cost me $5 each.

(As a side note, bookmark Fiverr once you get there. I use it for all kinds of things. The book you're reading right now was converted into the Kindle format for $5 by someone on Fiverr, and the book cover was designed for $5 by a different Fiverr seller. If you're reading this in a language other than English, the person who translated it for me was someone I found on Fiverr as well).

One small note of caution here: Just be careful on how non-standard you go on your resume design. There are a million design styles and I couldn't hope to cover them all here, and even if I could, design is always going to be a matter of taste.

There are tons of excellent resume designs on Fiverr, but there are also some I think are a bit over the top. Lots of people hate reading reverse type (light text on a dark background), so I steer clear of that. Others condense their resume onto something the size of a beer coaster, which is very creative and cool-looking, but probably too much for most employers.

You'll have to be the judge here of what's good and what's not. But a splash of color and good design definitely helps you stand out from your competitors.

GOOD GOD, CLEAN YOURSELF UP!
(OR, "BONUS INTERVIEW TIPS!")

This book isn't about job interviews; that's an entirely different book for a different day. If you've enjoyed this book and want another volume of my advice on that topic, let me know on my Amazon author page and I'll take up the job.

But I didn't want to leave you TOTALLY without guidance here on interviews. After all, if you follow the advice in this book about your resume, you'll be getting plenty of 'em. So I'll give you the basics here on getting your appearance right when you show up ready to kick ass and take names.

It's actually pretty ironic that a section of my book talks about personal hygiene and appearance, because those subjects were always sore spots with me as a rebellious kid growing up and still a free-spirited worker at the beginning of my career. I was a child of the 1980s and the hair-metal scene, and consequently I had long, headbanger hair for much of my youth. I was fired from not one, but TWO jobs for refusing to cut my hair.

And although the '80s weren't exactly the '50s, there were still plenty of people who very much frowned on boys with long "girl hair," not to mention earrings. And I don't just mean like little stud earrings, either. I mean like, giant, gold hoop earrings. I didn't give a shit. I was a ROCKER, man. If it's too loud, you're too old! HORNS UP, ROCK ON! (I'm still sort of that way, minus the hair and earrings).

I also grew up with a very "man's man" attitude about personal grooming. Metrosexuality and its aftermath had not yet descended upon Box Elder, South Dakota. Yeah, I took showers and wore deodorant, but many other basic staples of adult personal grooming escaped me. I cut my fingernails, but usually I had to be reminded. My hair was long and metal and unkempt, and a lot of my clothes had holes in them. My facial hair was different from one day to the next, and if you think I was paying even the slightest bit of tweezer attention to my unibrow, well, you had another thing coming. That was for women. Only.

You may have then asked me if those earrings dangling from my ears were also for women only, and I would've had to explain to you that not only were they not just for women, that they were *rad*.

These habits didn't change easily, but they did change eventually, at least during the job-search phase. And so must yours. Look, I'm not saying you have to change your stick-it-to-The-Man appearance forever; just long enough to make The Man comfortable enough to give you a job.

So here's a primer on appearance for those resume photos as well as job interview. Follow these basics and you'll be fine.

Hair (Men): Really, any hairstyle is fine, as long as it appears that you meant for it to look that way. Very short hair is pretty hard to screw up, so I'll skip that. For short-medium length hair, just make sure it's clean and brushed and out of your eyes, and you're fine. All you longhairs: you're fine as well, just make sure it's clean and out of your face. If you can't do that without a ponytail, put it in a ponytail.

The long and short of it for dudes in the hair department is keeping it out of your face. Make sure we can see your entire face, and you'll be fine.

Hair (Ladies): I know my place in life, and that place is not giving hair advice to women. I'm outgunned and outclassed. The only thing I can think to mention is that the occasional blue, purple or bright pink streaks (or more than streaks) are sometimes unwelcome in some arenas. Corporate gigs sometimes frown on them, and I know of more than a few hospitals who don't allow them for anyone: doctors, nurses, greeters, janitors, nobody.

Otherwise, you know way better than I what constitutes nice-looking hair. Let's put it this way: I've sat in hundreds of interviews in my life, and never have I thought, or heard anyone say, "She was great, except she really should've done something different with her hair before the interview." Not once.

Nails (Men): Cut them, and clean the area where the nails used to be with soap. That's all there is, it's very simple. But you'd be surprised how many dudes do one or the other but not both, or neither one, before an interview.

Your fingernails are one area that yes, all employers take note of. Dirty-ass long fingernails? Ugh. Not cool. Nicely clipped nails with the gunk underneath still there? Gross. Clean nails that are long? No thanks, werewolf. Clip them close and clean your fingertips, and you're golden.

And for God's sake, don't chew them during the interview, please.

Nails (Ladies): You've got plenty of leeway here. If you don't paint or file or manicure your fingernails, that's not a problem. You don't have to come to a job interview looking like you came straight from a spa day. Just read the above section about men's fingernails: make sure you clip and clean them before you show up.

If you ARE in the habit of fancying up your fingernails, make sure they're at least freshly painted enough that you don't have spotty remnants of polish all over them. That's a little sloppy-looking, and looking sloppy is the enemy of what you're after here. Go with a solid color — no rainbows or sparkle-storms or Hello Kittys painted on each individual nail.

And if you're one of those ladies who keeps exotic fingernails so long that it takes you 30 seconds to pick up a quarter off your kitchen counter: Cut them down to normal human length before you interview. Otherwise — and trust me on this — the only thing your interviewers will be able to concentrate on, and the only thing they'll remember about you, is your terrifying Edward Scissorhands fingernails.

And for God's sake, don't chew them during the interview, please.

Toenails (Men and Ladies): Trick question! Man or woman, your toenails should not be visible during a job interview. If you wanna show off your lovely pedi and six toe rings after you get the job, then fine — but not while you're trying to get it.

And for God's sake, don't chew them during the interview, please.

Facial hair (Men): Always a toughie, but even more so during this golden age of handlebar mustaches and hipster beards and their hundreds of variations.

The overriding principle here, as with the hair on your head, is that your facial hair looks a certain way because that's *exactly how you want it to look*. You *tried* to make it look that way. It looks that way on *purpose*.

So, if you have the aforementioned well-coiffed, exquisitely shaped handlebar mustache, then go for it. Same goes for beards: whether it's short or long or somewhere in between, is it managed, shaped, clean? Is the growth even (suggesting that yes, you actually care for it and craft its appearance)? If so, knock yourself out.

On the other hand, is it haggard and sprouting in all different ways, spotty in places, long here and short there? Does it look like you stash pens or joints or small animals in it? Can I tell what you had for breakfast by examining it closely? In any of these cases — whether you planned it to look that way or not — it's going to need help before your interview. You don't have to shave the whole thing off if you're married to the bearded life; just clean it up. Make it even. Wash the food and milk and booze out of it. Then you're good.

If you're in the middle of growing a beard when a job interview comes up but it's not quite filled in — shave it off for the interview and start over. Nothing says "I don't give a shit about this job" if you're not willing to set yourself back a couple of weeks of facial hair in order to get it. The hair will grow back soon, rest assured.

And if you're growing a beard simply to appear a little older and more seasoned, more experienced — don't. It doesn't work. A smooth face never stopped a guy from getting a job.

Teeth (Men and Ladies): Brush them as close to interview time as you can. Don't eat anything afterward, lest you be plagued by the worry that something's sticking in your teeth. You want to be able to smile easily and without fear during the interview. Ladies, check for lipstick on the teeth. That's embarrassing.

Makeup (Ladies): Three words here, friends: TAKE IT EASY. If you don't wear makeup, no problem, you don't have to start for this job interview. If you do wear makeup — and I know most of you do wear makeup of some kind — go light. Lip gloss, eye liner, mascara, then call it good. If you're going to do eye shadow, keep it subtle — skip the neon green or aqua or bright purple or anything else you might see in a Ke$ha or Christina Aguilera video, even if it's stuff that's contemporary and fashionable among your peers. And please, just say no to foundation and blush.

Fragrance (Men): Don't wear any. NONE. No cologne, and for God's sake, none of that goddamned Axe Body Spray or its knockoffs. You're going to a job interview, not to dance in a fleshy mob of 200 drunk people. A very popular e-card says it best: "Dear Axe Body Spray: Please put a suggested serving size on your bottle. Sincerely, Choking Girls Everywhere."

Fragrance (Women): If the allowable frangrancey-ness for a man is zero on a scale of zero to 10, it's no higher than 2 out of 10 for women. Please don't come heavily perfumed; I don't really want to smell you coming before you actually walk in the door, and I don't want to smell you for hours after you leave, either.

Here's some underrated advice for both genders: A clean human body doesn't smell like anything at all... and that's OK.

PARTING IS SUCH SWEET SORROW

(OR, "FINALLY, HE'S GOING TO SHUT UP.")

Here ends our journey, friends. You've got all the tools you need to go and mop the floor up with the other chumps out there who want the same jobs as you but weren't smart enough to buy this book and read it. Too bad, so sad. The strong eat the weak. Trample the weak, hurdle the dead.

I hope this isn't our last contact. Although I may sound like an angry dickhead when I'm writing, I'm eternally loyal to the people who buy my books, and I'm happy to answer any further questions you have about jobs, school, life, the universe, or whatever you want to ask. I may not get back to you in minutes because I have a company to run and books to write and occasionally my kids like to actually spend time with me, so I'm trying to enjoy that while it lasts before they become teenagers and start hating me except for when they want money.

If you're inclined to get in touch with me, here are tons of ways to do that:

www.facebook.com/joshua.barsch

This is my real, personal Facebook page. If you friend-request me, just mention you found me via this page in my book. If you actually bought this book then you're well past my "Facebook friend" threshold for me. My real friends rarely buy my books; they either already have jobs or are totally content sitting around and not working. :)

@judgejosh • *@joshbarsch*

Both of those Twitter handles work for me.

josh.barsch@gmail.com

That's my real email address. Drop me a line anytime. I'm probably busier than the average guy but it's not like I'm getting buried under a pile of fan mail, so I'll get back to you soon, I promise.

www.amazon.com/Josh-Barsch/e/B00GODGE3E/

That's my Amazon author profile. No one ever posts anything there, but who knows, maybe you'll start a trend.

Good luck on your job hunt. It's tough out there, but it's not insurmountable. Talented people who approach the job search intelligently (meaning, follow my advice in the book) always find a home somewhere. I hope it's somewhere you love and pays you extremely well. If not that, at least somewhere tolerable that pays your bills.

Happy Hunting!

Josh

REBEL
RESUME

CPSIA information can be obtained
at www.ICGtesting.com
Printed in the USA
LVHW081358311218
602282LV00013B/502/P